Emotional First-Aid for Children
Compassion in Action

As advocates for children, we endorse the philosophies of Dr. Dan Seigel for helping them feel safe, seen, heard and understood. Further, we subscribe to the idea that when adults show up for children, we help them develop trust that the world is a place that can be understood, and their interactions with it manageable, even during times of trouble. Children look to us to teach them how to react in a world that can be surprising and constantly changing.

Deborah D. Miller, PhD
Jondi Whitis, MToT

What People Say About
Emotional First-Aid for Children
Compassion in Action

"This is the best written, practical, up-to-date, straightforward instruction in Emotional First Aid for children of all ages that I would have liked to write, in the exact same way. Not reading it is immoral."
~ **Ulf Sandström**, *Hypnotherapist, Trauma Specialist*

"*Emotional First Aid for Children* is a very important book, not just for children, but for all of us. I think it should be required reading in every parenting class, and the concepts taught in schools on a regular basis.

Hopefully, we will never need the "preparedness" list in the beginning section about the family discussion. Some of these we have always done automatically, but every home should have this list posted where it can be accessed instantly, because, as the book says, *no matter what age you're dealing with, people are not at their best when fearful and confused.*

We would all be better able to deal not just with emergencies, but with everyday stressors if we practiced the techniques in this book.
~ **Nancy Gnecco**, *M.Ed., LPC, EFT Master, ACEP Diplomat*

"Deborah Miller and Jondi Whitis have written a much-needed guide to emotional first aid for children. What is particularly valuable about this book is its three-part practical and highly readable approach, which includes recommendations for self-care, instructions on how to care for children in traumatic situations, and procedures for teaching others how to help children in emotional distress.

The book is replete with practical strategies and techniques which blend time-tested psychological principles of social learning and behavior change with functional mind-body experiences that help children connect to the mechanisms of self-regulation.

I highly recommend this easy-to-follow manual to parents, teachers, therapists, and all those seeking to assist children on their journey to self-awareness and more peaceful minds and bodies."

~ ***Joseph T. Schippa***, *Ph.D., BCETS*
Clinical and School Psychologist
Board Certified Expert in Traumatic Stress
Director of Pupil Personnel Services
Edgemont Union Free School District, Scarsdale, NY

"Our young people need it, and we all need it, now more than ever. Times like these are both the best and the worst of times, when so much feels lost and hopeless and yet so many people are at their best: caring, sharing, rising to meet the needs of the vulnerable, following their inner wisdom, being who they truly are and sharing that selflessly and with unconditional love."

~ ***Heather Carter***, *UK*

"All children experience fear and sadness, but increases in anxiety disorders and depression are becoming endemic. Five times as many children are taking psychiatric medication compared to three decades ago.

What's a parent to do? *Emotional First Aid for Children* is a simple, practical guide that will teach you some of the most cutting-edge techniques parents can apply and teach their children for navigating through troubled times."

~ David Feinstein, Ph.D. Co-Author, *The Promise of Energy Psychology*

"Deborah and Jondi are two of my favorite trainers and practitioners in the world. They both speak with such clear voices about understanding trauma and how we can respond to it. This is especially true when it comes to understanding how trauma impacts children, and how they can be helped.

Emotional First-Aid for Children is essential for any parent who is concerned about the mental health and well-being of their children. It teaches how to respond to seemingly overwhelming problems with straightforward tools that any parent can use right away. Not only will this help your children, but it will help you as a parent to be happier and healthier."

~ Gene Monterastelli, Editor *TappingQandA.com*

"For parents & everyone who loves children, I highly recommend this book. Kids are growing up with unprecedented stress and pressures. It is taking a toll. Learn effective (& fast) practices to safe guard & enhance their mental health."

~ Kris Ferraro, Counselor, *International Energy Coach, Author, and Speaker*

Emotional First-Aid for Children
Compassion in Action
How to Quickly Help in Times of Trouble:
Practical and Easy-to-Use Trauma Relief
Techniques, Strategies and Interventions

ISBN: 978-0-9763200-0-5

Book and cover: designed, illustrated & produced
by Angela Treat Lyon. AngelaTreatLyonART.com
Copy edited by Deborah-Miriam Leff, PickyPickyPicky.net

Published by Light Within Enterprises

Deborah D. Miller, PhD.
DeborahMiller.org
Deborah@DeborahMiller.org

Jondi Whitis, MToT
JondiWhitis.com
Jondi@JondiWhitis.com

Compassion in Action

Emotional First-Aid for Children

How to Quickly Help in Times of Trouble

Practical and Easy-to-Use Trauma Relief
Techniques, Strategies and Interventions

Deborah D. Miller, PhD
Jondi Whitis, MToT

How to Quickly Help in Times of Trouble

Take a breath. Right now.
We can get through this, together!

Place both palms over your heart, covering the collarbones, and begin breathing as deeply as you can manage.

Allow this process to relax and open your chest. Visualize the breath flowing in and out of the heart. Continue for at least a minute, until feeling more calm.

NOTE: When we suggest you breathe to calm yourself *before taking action*, it doesn't mean you breathe for three minutes before taking action – it may just be 1 or 2 breaths!

What's in this book?

In this book you'll find three main focus areas:

- **First, take care of yourself.**
- **Next, care for the children in the traumatic situation.**
- **Then, teach others to help children.**

If you're troubled about something right now, stop reading and use the Comfort Hug.

Give it at least a minute to help you quickly rebalance and reset your system.

Being very practical, we'll focus on common sense ways to talk about and relieve the emotional and physical after effects experienced by a child following a sudden or challenging event. We want to do this quickly, effectively and gently in order to help prevent challenging events from becoming traumatic events.

By doing this, we help children avoid troubling after-effects that follow them through life.

Challenging events can be natural disasters, man-made (relationship dynamics, abuse, violence, stress or life changes within the family), or from the general environment (stressful events from work, school, community, war, politics or culture).

Our practical goal is to help you be more prepared for whatever life may throw at you.

This book teaches simple strategies and intervention techniques that incorporate breathing and grounding, along with helpful information for working with our innate human design when under stress.

> This book is *not* to *fix* you or your child, but to help you take practical, common-sense actions which will support you to better deal with whatever is going on within and around you, *right now*.

For more in-depth information on the research and science of these concepts, please see our Appendix at the back of this book.

What do we mean by Troubling Times?

'Troubling times' are any of the many challenging experiences that cause us to react with a fight/flight/freeze reaction.

All of these commonly create a 'threat response,' which is a way of saying that the situation has triggered the body's natural reaction to perceived or very real threats to our well-being or survival.

This book addresses traumatic events of all kinds. For our purposes, we call them Big T trauma and Little T trauma, (although for a person experiencing a traumatic event, size is irrelevant).

Here are some examples of trauma:
- Natural Disasters (earthquake, flood, tornado, fire, freak accidents)
- Man-made Disasters (car crashes, war, shootings, attacks, crimes, addictions)
- Family Disruptions (incarceration, drugs, addiction, abuse, removal from home, loss, separation, divorce)
- Medical (receiving a diagnosis, illness, treatment, death)
- Unsettling events at home, work or school that can cause lasting emotional wounds, like bullying, targeting or aggression.

Because no matter what is happening, we're ALL always looking for:
- A feeling of being safe, protected, cared for
- A feeling of belonging, being wanted
- A sense of worth, feeling valued, accepted, good enough...or better!
- A way to feel loving and loved
- A way to make sense of the world, especially when it makes no sense
- A sense of inner peace and balance
- A way to be seen, heard and appreciated
- One or more ways to move past simple survival, into healthy responses or actions
- Hope, for a better future

Preparedness

Everyone wants to be well-prepared for times of trouble. Ideally, you've already created a preparedness plan for your family or group. If not, it's never too late to address that, and you'll find a good start on such a plan (boxed below), along with helpful areas of discussion with your family, group, team or school.

Engage your family or group in a discussion of:

- Emotional First-Aid Techniques (many in this book!)
- Details of your geographic area and possible disaster scenarios (hurricanes, tornadoes, floods, explosions, home fires, etc.).
- Safe escape or waiting places in the home, school or workplace.
- Safe escape or waiting places in the community.
- Designated meet-up location with your family or group.
- List of emergency numbers and contacts (police, fire, EMS, 9-1-1 calls, etc.).
- Communication plan: Phone Tree, social media applications, contacts, etc.
- Any important info about your building (how to turn off gas, water, electricity).
- Have a First-Aid kit prepared with emergency supplies.
- A shelter-in-place kit (family records, identification copies, passports, insurance, healthcare contacts, medications, etc., recent photographs of family members, toothbrush or DNA swabs, if you have them).
- Plans for pets, including transport and medications.
- Information for your specific needs (glasses, contacts, prescriptions or medical directions for things like seizures, allergies, asthma or diabetes, epi-pens, etc.)

Even though no one likes to think about their children encountering trauma, the truth is that most children will be exposed to some kind of significant traumatic event during their childhood. A vast study from the 1990s speaks to that, called ACEs, or Adverse Childhood Experiences. More discussion about that later; the important thing to know right now is that the study calculated that over 60% of American citizens had at least one adverse (negative) childhood experience. In this infinitely more complex world, that percentage has surely risen substantially considering all of the traumatic experiences that have occurred since this study.

One of our goals as parents, caregivers, teachers and community members is to protect children as much as possible, and help them quickly recover from the negative effects of life (or ACEs) to whatever extent that we can, by working in both prevention and remediation. We wish for those children to avoid growing up and passing their unresolved ACEs on to their own children.

This book is specifically about adding *emotional well-being* to any preparedness plan, whether you've got one in place, or are working on it right now.

This book is divided into 3 basic, practical parts:

- How to Help Yourself
- How to Help Children
- How to Teach Others to Help Children

Section 1
How to Help Yourself

First, and always, you have to
HELP YOURSELF FIRST.

What does that mean?

To be of the most help, you need to be the grounded, safe, resourceful one who actually can help. So, FIRST THING, breathe, ground and center yourself.

How? See page 1.

In times of real, immediate trouble (such as an earthquake, for instance), your natural impulse is for simple survival - actions and behaviors that will bring you some sense of safety. We're assuming that you're not reading this book in those times! *(If you are, please go to page 98 and 100 right now.)*

And for those reading this book in calmer times, we can teach you how to consciously take care of yourself so that when those times happen (and even the smaller, everyday sort of events), you'll know what to do to help yourself, and be ready to help the children around you. Just like the airlines tell you before take-off, put on your own oxygen mask first, before helping others.

So where to start? Grounding.

Whether or not you are actually in contact with the earth (which would be ideal), Grounding means being consciously 'present' in your body and feeling calm.

There are many ways to do this, and no one right way. Several we recommend are provided in the Appendix of this book *(page 95)*. Even so, the most important ways will be the ones you can easily remember and actually do. Let's go through the general process right now:

Generally, 'Grounding' has three main components:
- Breaking the stress response with breathing, and
- Regaining your capacity to think clearly, and
- Taking appropriate action with learned resources or tools.

It's not complicated. Try it, right now:
Just breathe.
Now focus *more consciously* on your breath:
- Try deliberately breathing more deeply and slowly.
- Use a longer exhale than inhale.
- Do this at least three times.

Now put your full attention on your body:
Ask yourself simple questions like:
- How tight is my chest?
- Can I breathe freely, deeply and easily?
- Is anything wobbly or shaky?

Take a few more breaths, gently filling your chest, then completely release the air. Scan your body again; what do you notice, now? Are you breathing more deeply? Is your body more relaxed? If not, notice the parts that are still holding tension, and breathe into those parts.

This is the beginning of developing more body awareness - awareness of what being IN your body (embodied) feels like. Are you noticing the difference?

If not, take a few more deep breaths, with full, slow releases, until you do.

Once you start to breathe more deeply, oxygen will flow more freely to your brain - which allows you to start thinking instead of simply reacting. Now you can think and take better action on whatever situation is at hand.

Once you're truly thinking, you can access, recall and use the helpful information, tools and techniques shared with you in this book, and any other resources you've already learned and stored.

We're teaching you **Emotional First-Aid**. This is a useful beginner's guide to creating practical well-being and wellness-care. Take a look at four very different phases of challenging times:
- In the moment.
- As the situation unfolds.
- After the upsetting event has passed.
- Moving towards creating additional resources for potentially troubling times ahead.

All of us can be easily overwhelmed or distracted during troubling times. Some may even feel challenged by the very *idea* of being called upon to help others, especially frightened children. But one thing is always true: it's *always* best to start with yourself. We'll repeat this several times throughout the book... **Help yourself first.**

Why the Me First emphasis?

As we said above, you have to be mentally, physically and emotionally prepared in order to help others. That means being grounded and thinking clearly, so that your body and mind can work together to take productive action. That means developing a mindset, and learning practical resources that will help you respond. Survival odds greatly increase when we're prepared.

Remember the airline safety analogy? Every airline flight begins with safety reminders about putting on your own oxygen mask before trying to help others. We need blood and oxygen flowing to our brains in order to think clearly, and to remember the learned skills that will help us survive.

For instance, can you see how any of these situations would be better managed by knowing Emotional First-Aid ... and being grounded enough to remember to apply it?

- When we're overwhelmed or flooded by strong emotions (fear, guilt, worry, confusion, powerlessness, rage, injustice).
- When we're sick with worry for our children or circumstances.
- When we're faced with chaos, sudden or frequent uncertainty.
- When we're triggered by something that reminds us of our own unhealed places and memories.
- When it's difficult to think clearly or take appropriate action.

These common situations create bodily reactions, which we call stress response overloads. Again, invoking slower and deeper breathing is *the first, best thing* we can do to break that overload condition. As you begin to ground, you'll find you are able to think more clearly about the situation. You'll more easily see the various options and *productive* steps to take. In short, grounding yourself first immediately begins restoring your power and reasoning.

The Simple Science of Our Human Design

Let's turn our attention to a basic understanding of what modern science tells us - specifically, how humans react in times of great stress, prolonged threat or sudden shock. Humans have an inborn array of natural defensive reactions collectively called our 'threat response.'

To aid survival, the body's natural reactions to threat (real or perceived) is to begin heightening incoming sensory information, while simultaneously preparing for escape or defense. It does that by:
- Redirecting blood from our non-essential functions to our major muscles.
- Widening pupils and visual field.
- Amplifying our hearing.
- Increasing heart rate and blood pressure.
- Altering the sensation of time passing and slowing down, to record every possible pertinent detail we might need to make the best responses and choices.

This can feel very odd and disorienting, especially if there is no one to fight and nowhere to flee! But the goal is a better understanding of what the body is naturally doing, in order to be more prepared to move through this state with speed and ease, instead of confusion. Then you can connect with the interventions and recovery strategies you are learning here and will practice.

The Mind-Body Connection

The fastest growing health field is commonly called mind-body, or mind-body connection. That generally means understanding the interconnectedness between how our physical body *reacts*, to the way our mind *perceives* its environment or situation. Simultaneously, our human design includes a type of sensing we call *emotion*, which gives us even more information and clues about what we're seeing or experiencing. Taken all together we create a Body-Mind-Emotion information system, designed to help us not only survive, but *thrive*.

**It's not just what happens to us -
it's the *meaning* we give to what happens to us
that often is most important!**

The Mind-Body connection naturally synthesizes incoming information from the world, using our three information systems (Mind, Body and Emotions) to make meaning of the experience. Humans are natural meaning-makers. Making sense of things helps us survive. Thanks to a lot of research and study, it's now known that a person's interpretation of an event and the meaning given to it, are likely as important as the actual event itself.

14

Can you see how using the understanding of our design and information systems might help us survive? Thrive? A simple shift of perspective alone can jump-start the body's own natural healing processes.

About Those Things Called Emotions - What are they, anyway?

Emotions are simply energy in motion (energy + motion = emotion), containing helpful information to signal, remind or call us to action. They are neither good nor bad, they are simply *information* - very *powerful* information.

The emerging field of Epigenetics reveals our powerful, complex neurology and biological interconnectivity. Research shows that how one perceives the world - especially our perception of threat - has a large hand in transforming our biology, at a cellular level. This process begins in the womb, as the developing human is prepared for its outside environment. The same chemical 'mix' of emotions the mother's body is experiencing is 'fed' to the infant's biology, so that it prepares for the world after birth.

Now that you know this, it may be easier to accept the feelings and sensations called emotions by seeing their positive intention. It's part of our design! Emotion brings us information. Now you can help others understand how to use, rather than fear, their strong emotions.

Quick Review

First, we start with ourselves, grounding ourselves to take better actions and make better choices.

Breathe, ground and center yourself

Second, honor Emotions as information with a positive intention, and an integral part of our survival design.

Knowing that, pay more thoughtful attention to incoming information, and make better use of it.

Back to That Grounding Thing and Why It's the First, Best Step...

Basic Grounding

The most basic grounding techniques are simple breathing techniques and body movements that will immediately help you get centered and balanced. Of course, there are many ways to do this. No one has the final word on the correct way to do breathing exercises, as there have been many ways developed over time. But we've gathered those that work really well here in this book, to make it easy for you. Let's try another one, right now:

Tap *lightly*, just below the two collarbone 'knobs' under your neck. Use the tips of the first two fingers on each hand to tap. Breathe slowly in and out as you tap. *(See illustration on page 16.)* You can tap one or both sides, your choice.

Once you feel grounded, and notice you're thinking more clearly, ask yourself:
- What is the situation around me? What is actually going on, right now?
- What is 'mine to do?' (Which means, what can *I* reasonably and appropriately do, in this very moment?)

If you are still feeling confused about what to do or what is going on, we recommend another useful procedure. *(It's called the 3x3, on page 109 in the Appendix, along with many other useful strategies you might find very useful.)*

Get Into Your Heart (We call this Heart Breathing)

What does that mean?

The heart is more than just a blood-pumping device, it's also an information processing system that connects and communicates back and forth with the brain. Yes, that means the heart *talks* to the brain and vice versa. In fact, the heart has 40,000 nerve cells called neurites that function *like a brain within the heart* and independently of the brain! Our powerful hearts are recognized in Traditional Chinese Medicine as 'The Emperor.'

This communication between the heart and brain is key to our stress response and our ability to calm ourselves, feel empathy, be more intuitive and take heart-guided actions. Which means that the heart is a critical part of our self-empowerment response. Synchronizing how our heart and brain talk to each other expands our body's ability to operate from a bigger, more connected state, which can make all the difference in a crisis situation.

Focusing on the heart, and breathing from that heart-focused place, means we develop the capacity to connect and synchronize with our higher brain functions. The official name for this is Heart-Brain *Coherence* or Heart Brain *Harmony*.

We need this heart connection at the most *in*opportune moments - the unexpected, sudden, painful, startling, unwanted and distressful ones - like crisis or illness. The more we practice creating heart-brain harmony in times of calm, the more it becomes hardwired into our system.

This means we'll respond with heart-brain harmony *automatically* when it is needed. It's a different kind of preparedness - like practicing fire drills, we learn this in times of calm so that in the event of a real fire, we can *automatically* take appropriate action.

This hardwiring is another foundation of the Mind-Body medicine we spoke of earlier; it's a phase describing the connection and interaction between our physical body, mind and behaviors - and the powerful ways that it affects our health and well-being.

Right here, right now, we'll teach you how to take action from a better place than reacting out of a simple, innate survival mode.

How to Create Heart-Brain Harmony

- Shift your awareness from your mind to your heart - a simple touch with the hand to the heart area can be enough to begin the shift.

  - Breathe slowly for 1-2 minutes and consciously, as you develop an awareness of your breath.
  - Feel compassionate empathy (meaning feel with the person or situation).

When grounded, breathing, and connected in mind and heart, you have full access to your own resources, and you're ready to take action. From this state it's easier to know 'what is yours to do,' given the situation, location and your abilities. In other words, to know the *context* of the situation you're facing, and therefore, what is appropriate to do or expect yourself to do.

Remember: It's the DAILY PRACTICE that creates the ability to respond well to any situation that comes to us.

Have you ever heard the phrase, *whatever fires together, wires together?'* This describes how our brain's neurons begin creating new pathways of thinking and responding. Repetition is how we create patterns and habits that lead to an automatic response, for our brain to direct our body's reactions. Repetition is just a word for the consistent practice that creates a habit. That habit is actually a new, neural pathway that becomes automatic, even in times of crisis. This is how our brain 'learns' and 'remembers' and creates resilience!

Whether learning to walk, driving a car, tying our shoes, or escaping safely from a burning building, we need certain actions to become automatic. However, not all automatic actions are in our best interest - for example, overreacting from panic or anger, eating to find comfort instead of connecting with a loved one, hiding or stuffing down our truth, etc. It's possible that all of these were originally useful strategies, but when they became our automatic go-to habit over time, these habits became the opposite - really *un*helpful.

That's why getting to a state of Heart-Brain Harmony or centeredness, and consistently practicing grounding tools is a good thing - it's *WHAT YOU WANT to create*, versus simply reacting from old, unwanted or unhelpful habits. It's a shift from reactive to proactive.

We've only just begun providing helpful interventions for you; there are many more in the *Appendix* on page 95. Think of these as *common sense preparedness.* Later in this book (and in our full course), we'll go deeper, providing a full range of strategies for different situations.

Remember, it's okay to ask for help.

Even though we have expectations that we SHOULD KNOW what to do, and that we SHOULD be able to do everything perfectly, and ON OUR OWN, somehow...

- We DO know that is not realistically possible.
- *There is no such perfect thing.*
- There is only the *next best thing* you can do.
- Sometimes that means simply asking for help.
- We can ask for help as well as provide it.

Now that you have some basic techniques for taking care of yourself, let's turn our attention to how you can help others, especially children.

Children, whether our own or someone else's, are depending upon us to help, guide, reassure, and protect them.

Section 2
How to Help Children

Once you've become prepared by practicing what you've learned here, you can put the knowledge to use:
- You can get grounded to reduce your own stress and overwhelm;
- You can calm yourself by heart breathing, and
- Now you're ready to help others.

Who Are We Talking About?

Even though this book is specifically focused upon helping *children* who are exposed to sudden or troubling situations, the same concepts are true for the world at large. Whether during, or in the aftermath...*you can help.* As an adult or older caregiver, once grounded and centered, you will be ready to help children, other parents and other adults from panicking or further harm.

Children look to you for your reaction in order to learn how to handle the world.

Experts all agree that the number one priority for humans is to feel safe; that is doubly important for children. The second thing we're all seeking is assurance that 'everything will be all right.' In delivering these two basic reassurances to children, we need to consider what we *can* say and do, that is truthful, realistic and also accessible to them.

23

What does that mean?

This calls for expanding our focus, to incorporate a category of emotional first-aid called *Verbal* First-Aid.

Verbal First-Aid is an important feature of the Emotional First-Aid toolbox. To reach the children who need your help or support, you must use age-appropriate language and customize your approach to the particular child and their needs.

You'll notice in the first section of this book we were creating understanding for how to work *with* our natural alarm system and behaviors, especially what humans do when frightened.

Now we're adding to that, focusing on how to *express* to children proactive directions and necessary actions in a way that will be both accessible and easily followed.

So, what will learning *Emotional First-Aid* do for them?

The Emotional First-Aid toolbox helps children (and those around them) better manage what's going on during all kinds of situations, and to release the harmful effects that may arise from having observed or lived through challenges.

Truthfully, most children in the world will be exposed to some type of troubling incident or trauma in their lifetime, so you can be assured you are learning something very useful that will help them.

Let us be clear here: what we're teaching is not just emergency training! There are many opportunities when children need help to better handle common life events, such as:

- Health issues, including medical diagnosis and treatment.
- Success/failure, grades/achievement expectations, preparation and aftermath.
- Sports, school or performance issues, anxieties and doubts.
- Home trauma such as fighting, violence, substance abuse and divorce.
- School trauma such as bullying, intimidation or forced participation and peer pressure.
- An experience of trauma or abuse, whether present or past.
- Unsafe world experiences or events (war, shootings, natural disasters), including just observing those circumstances, especially chronically, as in news 'cycles.'
- Overwhelming emotional issues or feelings (current or unresolved in the past).
- Inherited beliefs, limiting beliefs, patterns and family or cultural 'rules.'

What exactly is *Emotional First-Aid* and How Does it Work?

By using these easily applied strategies and interventions, we can maintain our own mental and emotional groundedness that will then allow us to help others.

That's the first part of *Emotional First-Aid* - to be there for them, ready and capable of what they will need from us.

We can both model and teach children what we know and do for ourselves: how to effectively 'arrest' the body's natural stress or threat response, to return normal blood flow and oxygen to the brain, creating a more resourceful state.

We can teach them and allow them to experience how quickly finding that state makes helpful actions available to them, and more likely to happen.

We can allow them to experience how being able to return to a calm state quickly will create better, more positive choices, actions and outcomes. And that capability is never more in demand than in times of crisis.

In preparation for that, here are two principles that will always be true:

- First take care of yourself and your own reactions (yes, we are repeating this again and again, until it is second nature, or automatic).

- Second, strive to examine and release all past traumatic or troubling incidents from your own life, so they'll not be present or triggered in the future; triggering from unresolved past events will prevent you from fully helping children in their time of need.

- We're passing on a life processing toolset to use BEFORE you need to address an emergency or challenging situation. It's the perfect 'life-processor' for everything Life throws at us.

Accessing your learned skills and resources is easier than you think; we're reinforcing three points that we hope make good sense to you OR a child:
- Be prepared for purpose - your intention to be of help.
- Breathe purposefully: more slowly, more deeply, and with longer exhales.
- Create the heart-brain harmony connection within yourself.

ALL three bulleted steps have suggestions and instructions in the *Appendix* starting on page 95.

Overall, helping children weather demanding and troubling times *well* depends upon understanding the kind of situation they're facing, and what 'phase' of the situation they're currently in. What do we mean by that? Simply this:

At the very start, as an event begins to unfold, is a very different matter than DURING an event, which is quite different from the situation they'll face JUST AFTER an event has passed, and again even more different is the situation they'll be facing A LONG TIME AFTER the event has passed.

We smartly prepare and resource ourselves and our actions by learning to quickly assess which phase we're faced with.

ALL stages need these four elements to help us take appropriate, productive action:

1. Observing
2. Listening
3. Interpreting
4. Taking Action

These four elements help us develop an appropriate approach or action from the context of the current situation.

Take a look at these four basic elements that lead to natural action:

- **Observe** what requires immediate attention.
- **Listen** to what is being said, asked for or needed.
- **Interpret** what you hear is needed, and combine that with what is yours to do. If not yours to do, what or to whom it should it be passed?
- **An appropriate Action plan** organically flows from answers to the above three elements.

Let's break down this appropriate Action more specifically, after using those four elements.

You can see an organic and logical flow:

- Does the circumstance need a call to 9-1-1 (or your local emergency hotline number)? If so, and after an emergency services alert has been sent, ask next steps.
- Is the situation still playing out, right now, or are you witnessing or hearing about it after the fact?

- Do you have any specialty training that relates to the situation at hand? Are you an emergency services worker or licensed healthcare provider?
- What is your relationship to the situation and person(s): an innocent bystander? Your child? A school child? Parent? Teacher? Neighbor?
- Choose how to best communicate to the child/children, given your relationship AND their age/capabilities.
- What else does the child's situation seem to require, and can you provide that?
- If not, what is *the next best* appropriate thing you can do?

And even though we hope you'll *not* be in this position, consider: what if you're not in a place where you can call upon trained responders for help?

Some examples:

- Outdoors in Nature - camping, hiking or climbing, especially in a remote area.
- In water, such as an ocean, lake, or river.
- Caught in snow, ice, storm or flood.
- Driving or car trouble in a remote area.
- A lost child in a strange city, or on vacation, etc., especially with language barriers.
- Sudden onset of allergic reaction, illness, etc.

No matter what situation you encounter, you'll always be more useful by being prepared to take appropriate action with considered, informed choices and skills delivered from a calm, grounded state.

That's what this book is all about.

We've chosen tools and techniques in the *Appendix* (starts on page 95) that we've observed work the best with various age groups, and in a wide variety of situations.

Of course, no technique is effective if you don't use it or forget to apply what you know. So, what's the best way to ensure that?

Become and stay grounded.

> Often, the best thing we can do to help ourselves is to simply become and STAY grounded - Heart-Brain centered and present to ourselves and those around us.

When working with children, it's especially important to use an age-appropriate approach.

And in troubling times, it's even more important, as we want to reach them quickly. This is why we begin using *Verbal* First-Aid, as a part of our Emotional First-Aid toolkit. What exactly do we mean by that?

What *Is Verbal First-Aid* and How Does It Work?

Verbal First-Aid is the learned and applied skill of delivering deliberate and well-chosen words, phrases and directives to assist someone in fear, crisis or pain. These are the principles, that we'll share with you.

By thoughtfully choosing the kind of language you use, you are offering a type of care we call 'verbal first-aid' - the *deliberate use of your words* as a helping strategy:

- To quickly connect to the child, with your conscious use of body and verbal language.
- To move the child into positive action.
- To offer appropriate intervention strategies for the situation that will reduce and release both the emotional and physical stress of the moment.
- To reassure the child that you are present, supporting them, and will stay with them, at least until help arrives.

> What we say or hear in crisis has a profound effect, so use that information wisely to help yourself and others. What we say can make all the difference.

When we are in pain, fear or distress all of our sensory powers are heightened, and we become both more sensitive *and* more suggestible.

Added to that, we are biologically wired to seek and follow leaders, when in crisis. This is actually the perfect opportunity to offer children *Verbal First-Aid*: to suggest safe, immediate actions and lead others into productive action and into a supportive place, both emotionally and physically.

Reassurance is needed by every human in fear or pain, and even more so by children. You do *not* need to give false reassurance, however. *"I am here to help"* is very different from *"I'm sure everything will work out."* None of us can be sure of that, so we say what is true, and with conviction.

When offering *Verbal First-Aid*, avoid using long, run-on or complicated sentences, which are hard to hear or comprehend when people are afraid, in trouble or in pain.

Again, this is even more important for children. Abstract words or concepts cannot be easily deciphered when upset; in fact, it's hard to attend to *anything* when upset, so the best instructions to offer are simple, short and to the point.

Consider for a moment the difference between these two statements when addressing a frightened or overwhelmed child:

A. *"Oh, no! Pete? Oh, my, go through the gym, Pete. Bring your coat with you. Listen to me...why is the alarm going off? Hurry up, you need to move faster than that..."*
Or...
B. *"Pete, look at me. Take my hand. Let's go."*

Can you hear and feel the difference? Example B uses very simple but carefully calculated language to create safety by directing easy-to-follow actions for those in our care.

We want to reinforce three basic points from this section:

1. Create accessibility for the help you're offering by using words and terms children can easily understand and relate to in stressful moments. Short words, in simple sentences are easier to comprehend, and are key to better weathering a situation, both during and after the event.
2. Model healthy, safe reactions and actions to help children easily learn and emulate them. Your ability to be calm is essential in helping them both know they are safe and feel safe. Remember, you are taking advantage of their being 'hard-wired' to seek and follow a leader.
3. Give basic and believable emotional reassurance; use your strength and grounded support as they learn (or regain) their own strength and groundedness.

Let's look at a few examples of how those two concepts of *Emotional First-Aid* and *Verbal First-Aid* are easily combined.

First, we'll harness what you've learned about taking care of yourself, then put your skills to work helping others.

The Model:

- **For You:** Stop, get centered, breathe, assess, then help the children by speaking simply and directly
- **To Them:** Deliver short, thoughtful directives to help

them easily follow your lead. Provide truthful, simple reassurance that you are there to help them.

Using Languaging As a Tool

Since fear, confusion and lack of control create a sense of internal chaos, people often experience powerlessness and are at a loss about what to do. We can use *Verbal First-Aid* to help them move out of that state and back into a sense of personal control.

Any sense of control (for example, choosing to follow your breathing suggestions) can make a huge difference in how they will process, store and recover from troubling or traumatic events.

We'll focus on these two specific areas of *Verbal First-Aid* for helping and teaching others, and you'll then apply them to helping children during different phases of the situation at hand:

Two Specific Areas of *Verbal First-Aid*

1. Body Language
2. Using Words Strategically

1. Use Your Body Language to Communicate Safety

It's important to be aware that your body movement and positioning communicates volumes about your intentions, which in turn helps the child determine whether he or she is safe with you (or not!). Children constantly scan their environment for clues about whether it is safe for them - both the situation and the people in it.

Specifically, what does this mean for you? How does it look?

- How you position your body (not towering over them).
- How you move (not rushing towards them or suddenly getting in their faces).
- Your facial expressions (not signaling fear, danger, anger or short-temperedness).

Consciously creating and displaying non-threatening body language is an important key to create safety, long before you specifically address the child or group.

And, as all of our basic needs involve safety and connection, you can see how important it is to establish this right away, with the way you move and the pace with which you approach them.

Remember, especially if there is a language barrier, using body language strategically may be your first and most important tool!

2. Use Language Itself as *Verbal First-Aid*

Have you ever considered how people's words make you *feel*? How some people can make you feel calm or hopeful, and others can bring you quickly to fear or anxiety? What is it about them and how they express themselves that create that kind of feeling in you?

Be very conscious of:
a. Your tone of voice (calm, reassuring or comforting).
b. Specific pacing of your words (not rushed, run-on or garbled).

c. Age-specific, accessible, well-chosen words (simple, concrete, easily understood terms).
d. Very focused upon the positive action you wish them to take right now.

Here are three elements and examples of using language as Verbal First-Aid:

Directive: Short, easy commands.
Ex: Let's go now! Take your coats.

Factual: No-drama statements vs. an emotional reaction:
Ex: The alarm bell rang; let's go to our safe place.

Short: As few words as possible to think about or decipher:
Ex: Take your partner's hand. Walk quickly.

Here are good examples of using language skills to be directive, factual, and brief:

Parent, at home, hearing smoke alarm sounds:
First, deliberately breathes, then takes action by saying:
- "Mary, the alarm is ringing. Go to the door."
- "Carlos, grab my hand. Follow me."
- "Son, put on your shoes; we are leaving."

Teacher, at school hearing the signal for evacuation:
First, deliberately breathes. Then takes action, by saying:
- "Children, line up quickly; we're leaving the building."
- "Sandy, listen: make a line right here. Hold hands."
- "Kids, stop what you're doing. Follow me out of the building."

In a situation where you don't know anyone, but something has happened - i.e. earthquake, fire, traffic accident:
Take a deliberate breath. Then take action, and say:
- "Everyone, let's stay calm. I'm calling 911."
- "Is everyone okay? I've called for help."
- "Does anyone need help? Raise your hand if you need help."
- "Someone, call the police!" (or emergency support number)
- "Who is a doctor or nurse? Raise your hand if you're able to help!"

Reminder and Review:

Remember, no matter what age you're dealing with, people are not at their best when fearful and confused; they may react as toddlers do - immediately looking to a parent (or even the 'tall person in the room') for *their* reaction, then using it to gauge what their own reaction 'should' be.

Children look to us for leadership and safety. Handling the situation well is what will save lives, and goes a long way towards preventing traumatic encoding, by beginning to restore a sense of personal power and resilience.

Consciously considered and delivered words and actions are the model that the children around you will learn, copy and eventually pass on to others.

Combining *Emotional First-Aid* and *Verbal First-Aid* creates an effective and rapid strategy to manage any situation.

Combining *Emotional First Aid* and *Verbal First-Aid* Strategies

Let's combine what we've learned. There are things we can do (interventions, like breathing or physical holding) and approaches we can take (strategies, such as how we physically show up for a child, and what we say to them).

No tool or technique will help if we don't remember to actually use what we know!

The best tool in the world is only good when it's used.

Our goal is to teach you strategies and tools that are easily *learned and remembered*.

The younger the child, the more important it is to find something easy to do and repeat.

We're specifically focused on the tools that can be used to quickly direct their focus, help them calm their minds and bodies, and create safe, productive action.

For example, you could choose any of these easy strategies for children from the *Appendix*, page 95.

- Whale Breath
- Fingertip Squeezes
- 3 x 3 (*left*)
- Comfort Hug

Find these in the Appendix on page 95, or keep reading, and learn the strategies later.

With older children, it's important to treat them with dignity, offering age-appropriate explanations. Thoughtfully adjust the names of the strategies so they are more grown up, so they'll *want* to use them.

For example, an exercise like 'whale breath' can also be called 'volcano breath,' or 'dragon breath'. We recommend keeping language short and intentionally basic, to be easily understood by anyone.

A list of strategies and titles can look like this, for younger children, and another for older youth:

Younger:
Whale Breath
Butterfly
Heel Stomps
Tarzan Thumps
Shushing

Older:
Volcano Breath
Comfort Hug
Heel Stomps
Chest Thumps
Pretzel

You can go to the Appendix on page 95 right now to see these strategies and others, or keep reading to firmly integrate the conceptual aim of the work firmly in mind.

Another way to choose which strategies to use - and how to offer them - is to consider the 'phase' of the situation at hand. Combining the phase you're in with the three concepts we gave you earlier, help you better and more quickly decide what to do in any situation.

The four concepts again: Observing, Listening, Interpreting and then Taking Action.

Why? Because we're always looking for the answer to this question:
"What is the best and most appropriate approach, given the context of the current situation?

- **Observe** what requires immediate attention.
- **Listen** to what is being said, asked for or needed.
- **Interpret** what you hear they need, and combine that with what is yours to do. Is it yours to do? If not, *what or who* should it be passed along to?
- **Choose** an appropriate *Action Plan* from what you observed, above. An appropriate *Action Plan* organically flows from answers to the above three elements. Take action.

Do keep in mind that most of us, most of the time, are doing the best that we can.

Challenging situations can cause us to lose sight of this, but children will remember forever that you treated them with dignity and respect (vs. anger, frustration or humiliation).

Reinforcing the Basic Steps Covered So Far:

- Always take care of yourself first by getting centered, taking a deep breath, then assessing the situation.
- Next, establish a connection by consciously reaching out to create safety for the child.
- Then decide what you can do that would best support the children around you, both emotionally and physically:
  - Create an atmosphere to calm fear or panic using your body language.
  - Give clear, crisp directions.
  - If necessary, move the children to a safer place.
  - Organize the children to take specific, productive actions.
  - Provide emotional support using both *Verbal* and *Emotional First-Aid* in your approach and directions.
  - Treat the children with dignity, knowing that they are usually doing their very best.

Let's Add This to Your Knowledge Base:

How events unfold, and at what moment you arrive upon the scene, will determine the options available to you, what approach you can take and what is yours to do. We'll use the word *phases* to describe the different stages or times of an event. Each phase demands a different kind of response. Here are some specifics:

PHASE 1: Just Before or Leading Up to an Event

Often a situation presents itself well before we're consciously aware of it.

It's as if *a primal or physical reaction occurs* - but we are not consciously thinking. Often, it's an intuitive hit that makes us look around for danger, or a habit deeply embedded in our survival systems.

We tend to have physical sensations *before* thoughts, such as butterflies in the stomach, a sense of fear raising hair on the back of our neck, or a tensing of muscles. These sensations are signals of a sudden awareness that something is different, imminent or that our thoughts are troubling us.

In this phase, as soon as you become aware of these sensations, ground yourself, so that you'll be more prepared to meet whatever challenge is arising.

PHASE 2: As the Event Begins

This is the phase that brings a sense of **uncertainty** of what is to come, and heightens our body's sensory intake and response systems.

Examples are: sirens or alarms, earthquake rumbles, gunfire, or even coming upon a shocking scene or noise, all of which can trigger an overwhelming or out-of-proportion response.

Our body's natural survival systems begin heightening the amount of information and the intensity with which it is received, preparing us to take action.

Physical body reactions and sensations are *signals* in

warning or response to what is unfolding, prompting you to sort through the situation's various uncertainties, and narrow down the best possible courses of action open to you.

- Am I feeling a sensation of impending danger, or is it just that something is 'off'? Does the sensation grow stronger?
- What do I need to pay attention to? Do I see anything out of place?
- Is there actually something I need to do?
- Is it possible that calming and grounding myself is all that is required of me right now?

PHASE 3: During the Event

This is *immediate* safety decision time.

It's crucial to stay as grounded as possible during this phase. This is not to say you'll become comfortable, but you *will* be more aware, *less reactive* and able to take *positive action* from a conscious state, instead in a panic. And, honestly? It would be completely normal to feel triggered or fearful.

Here is where we can take advantage of the body's own readiness to respond - that's our survival instinct at work.

The body's design is to be prepared to help you respond quickly, and when grounded, use that response in partnership with making conscious choices. In short, we need to have enough readiness, and at the same time enough 'distance' from reactivity to appraise the situation and make good decisions. That is why it's important to have a daily practice of grounding and heart-brain centering.

Proficiency with these techniques will help you take mindful action when a situation arises, versus just relying upon the body's automatic fight or flight threat responses.

Once grounded, ask yourself more searching questions before initiating previously practiced action steps (like fire drills and exit strategies).

Emotional First-Aid can also be on your list of actions to take immediately. Consider these helpful questions:

- *What specifically* is going on or happening, right now?
- *What* do *YOU* need to do, *right now?*
- *How long* has this been going on?
- *Where* could you go or lead children, right now, for more safety?
- *What* is the intensity of the situation right now, and what is causing the most stress? (Is it life-threatening or just momentarily very stressful?)
- Is the situation clear-cut, or completely chaotic? (For example, children running from the gym in terror vs. an altercation between two boys in the gym). Is there anything you could do right now to get better clarity about this?
- What can you reasonably expect the children to do?

Following your lead is easy when swiftly moving down a hallway, but a very different story when needing brute strength or agility for lifting debris or scaling a wall.

In this stage it's crucial to keep yourself grounded while continuing to gather more information about the changing environment, and therefore your changing role and options for helping support the children around you.

The simplest of things will help you do this, like taking slow, deep breaths with longer exhales while making your inventory, which will help keep the nervous system balanced and cognitive function high. (More, always, in the *Appendix, page 95.*)

PHASE 4: Just After the Event

How long after? And how has that changed the issues you must now deal with?

Again, *how* we proceed is often determined by the context of the situation. Use your easy interventions, such as *Gamut Point Tapping*, (*Appendix* page 108) to help you stay grounded as you continue to monitor the situation. Ask yourself (and anyone else you find who is knowledgeable about the situation):

- How dangerous is it now to proceed, either traveling away from the scene or to begin clean-up or rescue and recovery?
- Has the danger, or perceived danger, passed - or might it return? Given that, what do I need to do, now?

- Who or where are the resources to help me and any capable children in this effort?

You might add on another tool or two, like *the Thumps*, while you continue to ask more questions to prepare yourself for the next phase – initial recovery.

- Am I physically safe? Who else around me needs assistance? Can I provide that, or am I still in search of extra help?
- If I'm not safe, do I have the means to call or signal for help?
- Is it safe to leave my current location?
- Where is the best place to go, given what I now know?
- What might I have around me that would be useful to take with me?
- Who is the most vulnerable or of highest need among the children? Who is available and appropriate to help with them?

PHASE 5: Initial Recovery Phase

In the initial recovery phase we can finally address the emotional and physical reactions from the traumatic event, both for yourself and the children around you.

If medical attention is unnecessary or already underway, now is the time to deal with the *involuntary reactions* that are common features of sudden shock or trauma. They can include physical, emotional, or psychological releases. Dealing with the sensory system - the array of sights, sounds, smells, and tactile feelings from the event - is now more possible. Most likely we were not *consciously* aware of these sensory aspects at the time since many of our normal processes are suspended during the threat cycle, such as the 'thinking level' brain and digestive functions.

At this stage, several more kinds of recovery strategies are now available to us, including individual and group intervention strategies or even therapeutic counseling, in groups or one-to-one.

Later in the recovery process, the focus will change to protocols that address the event on a deeper level.

Here is a short list of protocols appropriate for these later phases of release and recovery, including *Emotional First-Aid*, as well as the following:

- Head Hold
- Tension Tamer
- Flow
- Snap, Clap and Stomp
- Tap n Talk
- Trauma Release Exercises
- Somatic Experiencing
- Emotional Freedom Techniques

PHASE 6: Long-Term Recovery, Maintenance and Sustainability

Now that the most traumatic portion of the event is over, and recovery has begun, it's time to determine what steps will best promote *long-term recovery*.

Long-term recovery goals include maintaining a calm, grounded state of being *without* overwhelming emotions and troubling memories surfacing that could cause further traumatic reactions.

This process is about taking all reasonable steps you can to prevent children from being re-traumatized or triggered by related memories and sensations from the traumatic event.

In essence, this is a form of trauma-informed care (TIC), in that you are aware and actively taking care to understand affected children's feelings and behaviors that may be their best attempts at coping with what they've experienced.

Given that, now is a good time to check out the *Appendix* on page 95 for very basic information about the impact of trauma on our natural, human design.

Leaving children confused or isolated in their own conclusions about their sensations and reactions can be retraumatizing and it's often the *meaning* they've given the experience that will cause the most problems in their future.

Becoming familiar with trauma basics will help children better understand what has happened to them, and make better sense of any unresolved symptoms from the event.

Commonly called normalizing, its intrinsic value is that the knowledge that their sensations or feelings are shared by many others in such circumstances brings relief - and the truth, that they are not broken or odd or unfixable, is a relief in itself. And not least, this phase's goal is also to sustain that state of well-being, going forward.

We'd like to remind you that a well thought-out, practiced family/community plan and emergency kit is something that everyone should have.

(You can find a good starter preparedness list on page 6.)

With *practiced* skills, you'll have much greater peace of mind facing any challenge because you are prepared. Even a small amount of practice will make a huge difference in your confidence and ability to take care of yourself, your children, and others, too.

Practicing in times of calm, or when the 'stakes are low' is an excellent way to prepare for challenging times in the future.

We've mentioned earlier in this book the example of having fire drills. Practicing learning during calm times is optimal; for example, taking children to a busy store when the errand is unimportant gives you the freedom to practice enforcing your personal behavior rules, with very low drama.

Why? Because you are clear about the true nature of the outing and your goals, so enforcing the rules you've set is straightforward and easy. Teaching Emotional First-Aid is much the same.

Now you have a basic understanding of how events unfold and how they can become traumatic, but theory alone isn't as useful as picturing real-life applications.

Let's look at a very common, everyday example of what we've been talking about, and examine each event phase as it unfolds:

As you're shopping in the supermarket on an average day with your child, you hear sudden loud noises. Naturally, that upsets everyone. Not knowing precisely what is happening, you can apply the steps we've outlined, by event phase:

1. DURING an unfolding event:
- Breathe to center yourself.
- Look around you and assess:
  - What is happening that you can see?
  - Is your child hurt or becoming overwhelmed? Is anyone else?
  - Can you use your centered state to model helpful breathing for them, and use your verbal first-aid to keep those around you calm and focused?
  - Is it necessary to model and pass on any breathing intervention you've learned?

After applying in-the-moment strategies, such as the ones on (page 98), and with everyone accounted for, calmer and ready to move into further action, ask yourself: *What are the next, best steps to take?*

You might model for them one of the touch strategies such as *Comfort Hug (page 100), Monkey (page 103)* or *Finger Squeezes (page 104)* while the situation unfolds. You might also apply your *Verbal First-Aid*, providing clear, calm directives such as a safe way out of the store, leading your child, and others, out of the area.

Keep in mind you can repeat these *in-the-moment Emotional First-Aid* strategies as often and for as long as necessary.

Continuing our example, let's move forward, although still in the DURING phase:

Everyone is now out in the parking lot, accounting for their families, etc. You can continue to model and use these strategies that will help yourself, your child and everyone around you.

 Look first at your own child. You might notice wide or glassy eyes, which could indicate that the child is in need of some safe connection and intervention.

Choosing from the tools in the Appendix, page 95, you could use *Verbal First-Aid*, suggesting to your child to follow your lead, and model a strategy for them, such as placing *Hands On Heart,* or a bit of *Whale Breath* to bring them 'back online' - back to present focus with you, their safe person.

You might also reassure them: *"Jack, I'm here with you. Breathe with me, right now."*

2. Then move into a JUST AFTER phase example:

Let's say that first responders are on the scene, and there is no other immediate action needed on your part.

- What might you notice? You might see your child (or another) clinging, or reluctant to leave your side or shaking, beginning to display the fear and body chemicals that release when we're scared.

- Use your *Verbal First-Aid*; reassure them in a calm tone that this is normal, and it is their body helping them release the fear they experienced, and it is over now.

- You might encourage them to do a movement like the *Butterfly* or *Heel Stomps* to help their bodies release their pent-up flight-or-fight energy.

- You can also do breathing, like the *4-7-8 count style* (*Appendix* page 98). Don't forget comforting safe touch, like offering a hug or simply holding their hand in silent reassurance.

3. Later, JUST AFTER the Situation is Completed, perhaps at home, or in the days following the supermarket incident:

If you notice the child behaving in an unusual way - something that is out of character for them - it may be related to the incident and indicate that the child still needs to release some remnant of their threat response to the past event.

Our goal is to help them release that, along with any emotional overwhelm or worry, false conclusions or catastrophizing. Some choices might include:

- Invite them to do EFT with you (use age-related words).
- Ask gently probing questions about the incident which may still be bothering them.
- Offer *Verbal First-Aid* and reassurance, coupled with a strategy such as talking while simultaneously doing *Finger Squeezes*.

Paying conscious attention to the indicators the child displays can easily make the difference between simply surviving an event, and moving through and past the incident into growth and recovery.

We call this *resilience* - bouncing back, becoming stronger and wiser than before.

Keep in mind that children may need more help from you in the *aftermath* than they do during or immediately after an incident, with the exception of emergency services.

Support for the aftermath is about long-term trauma, which you'll find in our *Emotional First-Aid for Children Course* (see page 112 for more info).

You'll find a small collection of these 'bouncing back' ideas, below.

4. LATER, in the LONGER TERM RECOVERY phase...

About a week later, when you return to the supermarket, if you notice that your child is not reacting to anything, it suggests that the effects of the earlier incident at the store are no longer a problem or have been released.

However, if you *do* notice a reaction, such as the child is reluctant to enter the same store, or is repeatedly looking around, scanning the area, jumpy or behaving in a clingy fashion, decide upon a follow-up strategy from the ones previously mentioned (or in the *Appendix* page 95).

You *could* ask the child something like this:
- Is there anything bothering you, Rosario?
- I notice you're looking around a lot, Heather. Is there something you're worried about?
- Does being back in the store remind you of what happened last time, Tyrell?

Their responses provide the opportunity to select one of the strategies in the *Appendix*, such as asking them to join you in some simple *Heel Stomps* or perhaps *Finger Squeezes* while you both discuss whatever is happening in their minds or bodies.

When you return home, you could do a more in-depth strategy, such as *EFT*, focusing upon the remaining emotions, thoughts, body sensations or stated worries from the original store incident, or even reinforcing the child's newly-found strengths. Keep in mind that every child and situation may be different. Sometimes we are easily able to do this for our children, and sometimes that support is best provided by a professional, *not* by us. We have no way of determining how each particular child will interpret a situation. It's different for every child and person. But we can expect that the situations below could easily be interpreted as traumatic to a child.

Let's call these 'Big T' or 'Little T' trauma experience, and we'll describe what we might mean by that.

Big T traumas might include:
- Serious Illness or death of a child, friend, family member, teacher or even a pet
- Natural Disasters
- Shootings, Attacks or Wars
- Serious Accidents or Injuries

Little T traumas might look like:
- Being bullied
- Failure (or the perception of failure) in exams or sports
- Social Anxiety
- Consistently feeling like a failure in comparison to others

How do we recognize if more is needed?

And how might you recognize a child wrestling with those 'Big T or Little T traumas'?

Aside from observable physical injury, there are often things going on in plain sight that suggest children are experiencing more distress than they can handle and don't have appropriate coping mechanisms. For instance, take a look at the list of indicators below. You might observe (at ANY phase or time) these signs, indicating that there's more to be done.

Be on the look-out for sudden behavioral changes or reactions of any kind, that are out of character for your child, such as:

- Observable shaking.
- A shutting down or withdrawal or a sort of stunned silence.
- Wide-eyed stare or glassy eyes.
- Inability to move or follow simple directions.
- Escalating panicky behaviors.
- Clinging, hiding, rocking.
- Reversion to younger behaviors like thumb-sucking or curling up into a helpless or fetal position or even a regression like bed-wetting or changes in sleep patterns.
- Anger, outbursts or belligerence; hitting, attacking or aggressiveness.
- Loss of appetite or enthusiasm for favorite foods, activities or people.

Remember, unless you are trained in emergency services or are a healthcare professional, the procedures and interventions we're outlining in this book are for everyone's *everyday* use.

As such, there is no suggestion that we are diagnosing or treating complicated conditions. Rather, we are presenting tried and true, common-sense actions and providing tools for helping those around you in times of trouble.

How do you know if it's time to get professional help for all involved?

- You're uncomfortable handling this, and are 'telegraphing' that to the child.
- You're not finding resolution, despite your best efforts.
- You're too emotionally involved yourself to be of much help.
- You see that the symptoms keep returning.
- The child seemingly can't or won't accept your help.
- A family member or friend is also involved, and it feels too personal.
- You can sense the trauma experienced is deeper than the emotional first-aid you can manage on your own.
- The child asks for someone else's help, or is uncomfortable having you help him or her.
- Someone whose opinion you respect suggests more help is needed, either for yourself or for your child.

Even if we do the best we possibly can, sometimes we have to acknowledge that the situation (and its aftermath on the child) is beyond our scope of practice or experience. In that case, it's time to go to the professionals.

How do you know if you're 'finished' helping them?

Asking yourself the kinds of questions below will help you determine whether your job needs to continue or is finished, at least for now:

- What is your responsibility in this area, if any?
- Who is responsible or qualified to give follow-up support?
  - What information should you pass on, if possible, to any emergency support personnel, or follow-up caregivers?
  - Are those services already underway, or do you need to wait for them?
- Will you likely have contact with the children and people you helped, later on? Is there an ongoing relationship, and what is your role because of that?
- How could you suggest follow-up treatment for your child or others?
  - Even if you mentioned having some follow-up support at the time of the crisis, recognize that they may not remember what you told them, because of their distressed state. What else needs to happen or be repeated?

Now what? How do we help them get their lives back?

Once we're satisfied that we are 'done' with our training and intervention responsibilities around this event, how do we consciously address moving back into normal life routines for the children?

And what, if anything, might be in the way of that?

There are two very common things that may occur:

1. The children's *unresolved* traumatic event history is triggered by the energy of others around them.

2. The children's *unresolved* stress reactions to recent events can be triggered by any of the aspects similar to things they encountered before - especially sensory aspects, such as sounds, sights, smells and even how their bodies were or are positioned.

For these two reasons, it is important for them to resolve and release their emotional experiences so that they are not accumulating more layers of stress reactions.

If we don't help them find a way to release the stress, aspects from these memories can easily trigger them later, and actually hamper their ability to take action for themselves or others around them.

In what is known as *'Vicarious Trauma,'* our own reactions to others' experiences can trigger strong emotional responses in us.

So even simply observing, hearing about or being around others that have been through a lot can become traumatic, therefore it's important to resolve and 'let go' of our own emotional responses and teach children to do the same.

This is commonly called 'doing our own work,' a form of self-care. Equipping children to do this early on is a wonderful gift for their present and their future.

When we consciously process and release our emotional and physical responses to an experience, we signal to the mind that the event is over, that we have survived and are safe; that is how we grow in what is called *resilience*. Our minds and bodies use the accumulated information gathered from our experiences to create better responses for *'the next time'* such a thing occurs.

If instead we allow them to 'keep' stressful experiences and responses 'alive,' the mind and body perceive the action to be ongoing.

This creates chronic stress, setting both the children and ourselves up for exhaustion, burn-out and potentially serious illness over time.

This can happen if we're not able to signal 'this event is complete' to the body (and specifically to the hippocampus area of our limbic system). The gathered information and responses are not shuttled into long-term memory. This means we have *reduced* capacity to be fully present, and able to cope with future stressful situations.

Need an example?

Let's say a parent with a child in the hospital (or even visiting a hospital setting) could easily accumulate vicarious emotional and physical traumas if not routinely using self-care release techniques.

Being around serious and challenging health issues, often matters of life and death, can have a serious effect on everyone's health. Restated, unprocessed and unresolved traumatic memories and responses can remain active, which means they can be triggered, leaving the parent far less capable of supporting or helping their child. Some potential triggers:

- A child can be triggered by another patient suffering in a way that is similar to their own experience.
- They could have been on the receiving end of strong emotions like fear or rage from a reactive family or patient, reminding them of something they previously experienced.
- An unconscious identification with an issue playing out before them, such as domestic violence or verbal abuse, triggers their own unresolved trauma reactions.
- Observing someone else's suffering and helplessness, they are reminded of another situation where something similar had happened, or their own sensations of helplessness.

So, how do you make sure you've helped them process and begin resolving their own previous experiences and reactions?

Using what you have learned so far about human design and stress reactions, you can take some of the simple actions below to help ground, rebalance and make sense of what you have accomplished, teaching children and those who support them to:

- Tap on the *Gamut Point* as they breathe, or give themselves a *Calming Hug*.
- Mindfully reinforce that the event is 'over,' they've survived and are safe.
- Consciously place focused attention on what is 'yours to do' and what is not.

- Reinforce the knowledge that they could, and focus upon anything they were able to accomplish.
  - Take compassionate pride in their ability to take care of themselves and support those who need their help.
  - Remind them that continuing to carry the stress of a situation is *not helpful* to anyone – neither the helper nor the helped.
  - Realize the experience has left them wiser and better able to manage any similar circumstances in the future.

This is the path to moving forward into Resilience.

Remember, as we described in *Section 1: How to Help Yourself*, humans are designed as a three-system model of Mind, Body, and Emotional information.

Consciously using this knowledge helps everyone close and complete the experience. We can engage the parts of our brains that process words by saying out loud what we notice, and often the simple truth is the perfect place to start.

It's useful to look at this through example. Here is a common medical situation to illustrate the point:

Let's say that you have managed to get sick children to a medical care facility. Now that the professionals are working with the children, what do you do with all your heightened emotions and reactions from the mad dash to get the children help? How do you begin signaling to your body and mind that a new phase (and new actions) are necessary to prepare for the next step of taking care of the children, after the doctors determine nothing more is needed?

Here are simple, easy ways to inform all three information systems (Mind, Body, Emotions) that a new phase is happening, and therefore your initial job is 'done.'

Try out these suggestions for each processing area:

Mind: *"She's in good hands, now. I know I did what I could. I did a good job with that and my job is done; I did my part, and it's done.* (Focusing the mind on the completion of the event.) **Body:** *Breathe, exhale fully, and shake it off; use the Heart Breathing hold to soothe yourself and focus on consciously feeling the body relaxing from the tension being held.* (This signals to the body that it is 'over.')

Emotions: Ask, *"What am I feeling as I look around, now that the crisis has passed?"* If you still feel any stressful emotions, you can choose an emotional release technique such as *EFT*. (Feeling calm indicates the body has released the emotions related to the situation.)

You might encourage yourself to further connect to your emotions, thoughts and physical body by placing your hands over your heart, following the *Heart Breathing* technique on *Appendix* page 102.

Even though it's *likely* there will be more to do, remind yourself and those helping you that the initial danger is over, and their bodies can now return to calm.

The body's natural recovery and restoration system is designed to learn from every circumstance, building resilience for the next event.

Resilience simply means our innate ability to bounce back after surviving a stressor, and learning from it. And we build resilience by living and surviving well!

Emotional First-Aid and Verbal First-Aid are ways of helping yourself, those you've trained and children to better weather an experience, and help prevent an event from being categorized as a 'traumatic experience,' which could, later become a 'trigger' or create avoidance behaviors.

What's the Best Way to Remember All This?

Practice!
Preparedness comes from practicing skills.

Breathe, ground, get heart-brain centered using favorite tools in the *Appendix*.

Take steps to free yourself of any post-event emotions or trauma you have picked up while helping others. Each of us will probably encounter something like this at least once during our lifetime.

Everyone will experience new circumstances that are

less than perfect, sudden or surprising in a troubling way, so it's a given that what we'll need in times like those is Preparedness, which is just a matter of taking conscious, practiced action.

Having gone through the above response and phases section, what are the takeaways for actions you can undertake in your own family, group or team in order to be response-ready?

A Beginning Check-List

- Do you have an updated first-aid kit in your house? A 'dash' bag to grab and run?
- Do you have a list of emergency numbers handy (written or in your cell phone)?
- Have you created a 'calling tree' or social media network to inform others?
- Have you created a local group of support - be it family, neighbors, etc.?

These are all measures to have taken beforehand, which is what preparedness is all about. If you don't yet have a plan, see our box on page 6 for a good start.

For more on how to help children and others move past upset and traumatic incidents, we hope you'll want to look into our comprehensive course, *Emotional First-Aid for Children* (see page 112 for more info). In it, you'll find more in-depth information, resources and wide-ranging conversations about supporting children into safe recovery, creating resilience and sustainable self-care practices.

Despite Our Best Efforts

It shouldn't surprise you to learn that, despite our best efforts, not every situation or person is within our capacity to help. And further, not everyone is open to being helped, or in their state of shock, capable of accepting our help, even though they may need it. (Sometimes, it is worth noting, our need to 'rescue' may be more about ourselves than the person or the situation.)

Some examples of when it is beyond our ability or current training to be effective, are when we are dealing with the following:

- Someone who is mentally ill or suicidal.
- A child or teen who is angry, reactive and impaired by drugs or alcohol.
- Abusive or violent situations involving children, which may include weapons.
- Medical emergencies and professional rescue operations or police actions in progress.
- Environments where you are under-equipped or unprepared to help a child or teen, such as dealing with treacherous ocean undertow, when you are not a strong swimmer, etc.
- And when the person, of any age, clearly says NO, and refuses our help.

So, what *could* you do, in situations like those?

Sometimes the best thing to do is ... *nothing*, if not qualified or confident to handle the situation.

In those instances, it is best to stay calm, grounded, and out of harm's way versus creating an obstacle to others who *can* help.

Keep in mind that there are things we do not know about a person such as their history, and whether they are responding from an injury or medical condition, current or past mental or psychological distress, etc.

There will always be some situations we couldn't possibly know about or be prepared for.

In those cases, simply observing the situation and creating a safe environment around the child or adult may be the best thing for you to do for them, *after* alerting the appropriate authorities that DO know what to do.

For instance, in the case of someone having a seizure, unless you're trained for this, the best thing to do *after* alerting medical responders is to keep the area around the person uncluttered and other passersby out of the way.

Now that we know how to take care of ourselves and help the children around us, the next topic is how to then take all of this knowledge and use it to teach others these skills, how to use them, and then pass them on.

Section 3
How to Teach Others to Help Children

After learning about helping ourselves first, then the children around us, we come to the inevitable desire to help teach others how to do the same.

This section explores using what you learned, and taking those concepts forward, in teaching others how to help children, too.

As we mentioned before, the resurgence of interest in and understanding of the 1990's Adverse Childhood Experiences (ACE) study, along with advances in our collective understanding of trauma treatment, means that we now have the opportunity to do better by our children.

Learning more about these areas, and putting this knowledge to work, is what we functionally mean by 'becoming trauma-informed.' Maybe you've heard the phrase 'trauma-informed,' or 'TIC': *Trauma-Informed Care.* But without context or application opportunities, it's hard to see what that has to do with each one of us on an everyday basis.

We start with context: teaching others how to help themselves by becoming more trauma-informed, then deliver care based upon their deeper understanding.

Here's how we think that works with our particular mission: 'Trauma-Informed Care' (TIC) means treating the whole person by taking into consideration past trauma, situations and the resulting coping mechanisms that may result from them.

When helping an individual, it means creating safe physical and emotional environments for not only the individual needing support, but the others involved and for those providing the support, in order to reduce retraumatization.

**There are Five Guiding Principles to TIC:
safety, choice, collaboration, trustworthiness
and empowerment.**

Adopting a trauma-informed care *mindset* helps us provide appropriate assistance and support.
It's a consciousness that informs our approach, delivery and application of whatever help we're offering.

It creates and maintains a focus upon safety and accessibility when delivering information, tools and techniques.

It is being mindful of possible past trauma.

A TIC mindset guides our choices of tools that are
> 1. conducive to recovery,
> 2. assist in reclaiming a state of well-being, and
> 3. promote resiliency.

So, how does one begin creating and using a trauma-informed mindset when teaching others?

Why Teach Others?

What's *your* goal for them? (Notice we did not say 'agenda.')

Four reasonable teaching goals with this TIC mindset might be:

- Train others to empower children by teaching them easy self-care skills to address the many circumstances they will encounter in their childhood and beyond.
- Create a greater conscious awareness of a group identity (such as a team, family, school, community). The group can work together in support of one another, through life's ups and downs.
- Co-create a world where people better understand their natural design, capabilities, the power and purpose of their emotions, and use that information to better survive adversity and promote rapid recovery.
- Create an ever-widening movement towards self-care and other-care that is easily taught and passed on.

First Things First:

Who are you going to be teaching?

As you've already seen, you can accomplish more, and much more easily and thoroughly, by adapting your techniques, language and approaches specifically to the 'target audience.'

What is the Context?

Are you addressing a current situation or is your goal to teach prevention and readiness?

THE WHO:

Let's divide potential target groups into three main categories:
- Older children who will be helping their peers, either one-on-one or in groups.
- Adults who work with children, either one-on-one or in groups.
- A mixed group (all the people that happen to be together in the situation).

Then consider each groups' current skill level:

1. Those who are ready to learn how to begin taking care of themselves and others, in better, healthier ways than they've learned to date.
Ex: Kids, Youth, or Teachers, Nurses, Social Workers, Day Care Providers, etc.'

2. Care Providers, etc.
Those who already know EFT or Energy Psychology techniques and want to *add* more tools and skills, such as *Emotional First-Aid*.
Ex: Students, Kids, Youth, or Practitioners, Therapists, School Psychologists, Coaches and those with a lot of practical experience assisting children.

3. School Psychologists, Coaches and those with a lot of practical experience assisting children.
Those who have need of these tools and skills, but may still be in the process of resolving something that's recently happened to or around them, possibly even with those who are still suffering.

Dealing with the aftermath of a situation is very different from dealing with an ongoing situation.

For example, consider how people in the following wartime scenarios require different approaches to address their trauma:
- Those who may be experiencing vicarious trauma from observing an event.
- Those in the aftermath of a traumatizing event.
- Those currently living in a war zone, such as an impacted school or city.

All of which is talking about the CONTEXT of what and who you'll teach, and therefore HOW you'll present your material.

THE CONTEXT:

- What situation are you in? *Is* there a situation at hand?
- Who you are teaching is one factor; where you are teaching is another.
- Perhaps even more importantly, what is the goal of those involved?

Those involved might include:

1. Teachers learning how to help students with the natural Big and Little T traumas of life commonly encountered at school.

2. Youth leaders who already know how to us EFT, but need more strategic interventions they can utilize when their community becomes overwhelmed or distressed by local events.

3. Practitioners of any age (who may also be social workers, teachers, special ed/needs professionals, hospital personnel, psychologists, therapists, nurses, physicians, para-professionals, school aides, caregivers, as well as other occupations we don't ordinarily think of, such as coaches, business leaders, and athletes) that see the need and use of Emotional First-Aid in everyday settings.

Re-Stating this - yes, it is that important:

**WHAT we teach will always be
a combination of two considerations:**

**WHO are we teaching.
The CONTEXT of their situation and need.**

No matter who you've chosen, and no matter whom you may have found yourself working with, we're repeating the general list of things you must address to keep everyone safely connected and you, as the teacher, grounded:

- Take Care of Yourself First (get grounded first thing, and throughout). Be fully present to the moment and capable of embodying and deploying your resources.
- Recognize what is yours to do, given your capabilities and training.
- Remain mindful of the present (the current phase and context of the situation) as well as the changing dynamic of the situation.
- Find or create Safety - a place that is out of harm's way and can support the children to be able to listen and take direction.
- Deliver an appropriate amount and depth of knowledge for the those being served.
- Be open and aware of others' reactions to the situation and adjust to suit the situation.
- Model your own groundedness, well-being and knowledge to those you are working with.
- Provide liberal and frequent opportunities for questions and supportive reinforcement.

WHEN:

An important part of teaching others is recognizing WHEN to approach the situation. As we showed you in Section 2, there are several distinct phases of every event or situation, and knowing how to recognize each is crucial to being effective.

Optimally, the question "Are they ready?" is often about one of these two things:

- When they are NOT overwhelmed (in fight, flight or freeze mode).
- When they are receptive to help or welcoming your support (which may be a function of what they perceive they need at any given moment, or a function of their ability to trust you to provide help/support).

Teaching others is an activity more likely done in later phases of recovery. We'll emphasize those in this section, and just briefly mention the other, earlier ones to refresh your memory.
(All are detailed for you in the Appendix, page 95.)

It is when you are in phases 4, 5 and 6 that you will likely be able to teach or train others.

Until that time, phases 1-4 are likely focused simply upon surviving the experience, not learning strategies.

- PHASE 1: Just Before/Leading Up to…
- PHASE 2: As it begins…
- PHASE 3: During…
- PHASE 4. Just after? (How long after?)

AFTER you've established that you are physically safe, perform the easy, basic interventions we've shown you, on yourself.

Beginning with PHASE 5, after the imminent danger is gone, is the right time to begin learning more about what has happened, how it may have affected them, and how one might best deal with it.

These include using tools like *Comfort Hugs* or *Gamut Point Tapping* to help you stay grounded. This is like the ripple in the water: it may attract interest, and you can begin teaching those same interventions to others.

PHASE 5. Initial Recovery Phase - After Incident Completion

In this phase you become the teacher. *Part 3* of this book is about teaching others how to, in turn, teach more people.

Point out how to notice additional needs to be addressed. Breaking this down into specifics helps, as it may not be obvious until one is taught to look for it:

To look for and attend to any medical or physical needs. Learn to assess sensory overwhelm and emotional states. Create a compassionate mindset - understand that it is possible past traumas are being triggered by the current situation.

Be aware of the basic differences between teaching children versus adults, or professionals versus the general public.

If medical attention is unnecessary, already underway, or not in the yours-to-do category, now is the time to teach about the involuntary reactions caused by a sudden shock.

Remind them that shock for a child is different than for an adult. Children react more instantly, and have less real-world experience to weather sudden traumatic events.

Teach other adults to deliberately move to a child's eye level, give reassuring looks, perhaps a light touch on the shoulder, and even a listening ear. These can make all the difference in helping a child to naturally release their emotional overwhelm, versus encoding the event as traumatic.

Teach others about the sensory system's heightened function during fear or threat: that it records the sights, sounds, smells, and touch from the event. The body takes it all in.

Recovery strategies may include using physical, emotional, or psychological release techniques which you'll find in the Appendix, starting on page 95. Teach the adults to help children use simple visual, practical, hands-on demonstrations to release their upset.

Teaching others to teach children can take place in a variety of ways: individual and group intervention exercises, or in therapeutic counseling (either in groups or one-on-one).

Protocols

Here is a short list of protocols helpful specifically for these last two phases of release and recovery. These are addressed in greater detail in the complete *Emotional First-Aid for Children* course *(see page 112 for more info)*:

- **Emotional First-Aid**
- Tension Tamer
- Flow

- **Trauma Release Exercises**
- **Somatic Experiencing (and similar body releases)**
- **Emotional Freedom Techniques (EFT)**

Traumatic events tend to render us 'helpless' or 'powerless.' Using *Emotional First-Aid* at this phase begins to re-empower us all.

We can each only do so much, but we're reminding you that a little bit of preparation and effort will make a huge difference in your confidence and ability to teach others to care for themselves, especially children. The benefits ripple outwards, as those who learn from you reach out to help others.

Practicing the skills will give you peace of mind because you'll be as prepared as you can be.

Perhaps even more importantly, it will make a huge difference in the childrens' sense of confidence in your ability to take care of them.

Later, they will be more confident in their own ability to take care of themselves and keep themselves safe. Reinforce the fact that children feel reassured and empowered when given appropriate knowledge and a role, such as participating in the family or group preparations for emergency.

When, in your teaching, you model grounded behavior coupled with your confident, practiced skills, you reinforce resilience.

Frequently remind those you've taught how well they've used their cooperation and new knowledge to come through an experience safely.

Not surprisingly, we remind you to teach others that a well thought-out (and practiced) family or community plan is something that everyone should have, as well as an emergency kit. *(The basic preparedness list is on page 6).*

Teach your students to think of this as a comprehensive 'fire drill' for their home, building, neighborhood, local school or community.

Phase 6. Long-Term Recovery, Maintenance and Sustainability

Once the traumatic event has passed, and recovery has been in progress for some time, the next teaching step is determining the actions that will promote long-term recovery.

During this phase we'd like you to teach others steps to prevent re-traumatization or triggering (by using the Emotional First-Aid interventions), and how to encourage and foster the development of resilience.

What do we want to teach you so you can help children sustain a state of well-being? In our course, *"Emotional First-Aid for Children,"* we'll train you in techniques that will help children maintain a calm, grounded state of being, resolve their troubling or overwhelming emotions, and, ensure that memories do not resurface and recreate reactionary trauma responses.

We teach compassionate 'students' like yourselves to help children better understand themselves and what has happened to them. This greatly assists them in making better sense of any unresolved symptoms or sensations from the event.

It's also a good time to ask the children about any conclusions they've made about themselves, the event, or even life. This is generally called normalizing the experience, a term for developing a good perspective and orientation between the event that happened and the present, safe environment.

It brings children relief to know that:

They are not the only one.
The feelings they are having are expected in such circumstances.

We'd like to see those working with children help the youngsters understand how troubling events can impact us all. If we don't teach this, the children may get stuck in feelings of isolation or confusion, and their unresolved sensations might create retraumatization.

How to tell if the strategies you teach are working:

- It can be as simple as understanding that when a child feels better, they will leave to 'go play' or another activity they like. (Often adults misinterpret their reasons for leaving.)

- Body language - a relaxing, or less tense appearance, especially in the facial expression around the eyes, more eye contact, or closer proximity.
- Seeing a smile or change in expression on their face, perhaps even hearing a statement that they feel a sense of relief. ("I'm okay, now.")

NOTE: Good news! No matter what phase you're in, they ALL involve beginning with grounding yourself, and becoming stable and calm before proceeding with the interventions. Each phase is best addressed with interventions that build from the simplest breathing variations all the way to multiple step methods.

If you wish to go deeper, please consider our comprehensive *Emotional First-Aid for Children course.* A link for more information about the Course is on page 112.

Reminder:

The *approach* we use in teaching others is almost as important as *what* we teach them.

Where to Begin?

Just as we've taught you in earlier sections:

- Remember to use a grounding and self-regulating intervention on yourself before presenting new material you want to teach.
- Tailor your approach to your demographic (age, profession, culture, language or common concerns).
- Pace deliberately, with condensed directions in small, accessible pieces.
- Stair-step the teaching, from simple to more complex information and movements.
- Remember to engage the group you're teaching on multiple sensory levels. Different people have different learning styles and sensory intake preferences, so use a combination of visual, auditory, and kinesthetic teaching methods. *(More on this in the full course)*

Remember Your Teaching Goal

Even though every person and situation is different, creating a state of calm self-regulation will help everyone better manage the aftermath of any troubling event. Our job is to model how to quickly and easily create that state and then teach others to do the same. That is successful teaching!

Although learning styles differ and deserve consideration, people of all ages learn best if you notice and address their immediate needs first. (School food programs were implemented to address childrens' hunger before the school day began for this reason.) By acknowledging or meeting the childrens' immediate needs, their capacity and enthusiasm for receiving new information increases.

So, first look to obvious needs, and creating a comfortable environment:

1. Needs
Is your group hungry, tired, thirsty, hot or in need of bathroom relief, or a place to sit?

2. Assess and Reinforce the Elements
After addressing immediate needs or obstacles to their comfort, reinforce the four elements you're teaching. These will help them determine the next, best positive action steps to take in any situation.

3. Observe
What is really going on? What do you see?
Are the children upset?
Is it difficult to carry on a conversation with them?
Are they glassy-eyed or shut down?
Are their conditions causing them to be distracted, too cramped, or even isolated?

4. Actively Listen
What is being said or left unsaid in reaction to the situation?

5. Interpret
In other words, make useful meaning from what you've seen and heard.

6. Take Action
Your positive, helpful actions come from the first three elements.

No matter what the circumstances, EVERYONE can be taught to use specific, easy-to-remember tools and skills that help them Self-Regulate (also known as Self-Calm or Self-Soothe).

Helping them to do this on their own will make a huge, positive difference.

Once learned, children naturally teach others. Once they're taught how to use *EFT* to self-soothe, they will easily pass along the knowledge to others.

We will train you to teach them how to use *Emotional First-Aid* that will help them connect, self-soothe, reduce stress and worry, and relieve suffering, no matter what happens in their lifetime.

Once calm and grounded, anyone can do a better job of everything.

REVIEW

- Children need to know and feel they are safe
- It all starts with YOU. That's why you need to be informed and ready before sudden or overwhelming events occur.
- Children take their cues from you, and how you are reacting in the situation.
- Children develop trust from the signals you are sending them, which includes your words, movements and actions, while showing them respect as fellow human beings.
- Help is not truly helpful unless it's used. Make things accessible and memorable.
- Customize your approach and manner of addressing them. This is key. Consider:
    1. who they are
    2. where they are / in what situation (context)
    3. their developmental and cultural ability to understand you
    4. that the children are likely doing the best they can

REMEMBER:

- Always move towards safety. (Physical, Mental, Emotional)

- State simple facts, without judgment.

- Planning is not being paranoid, nor inviting disaster.

- Connect, don't isolate.

- Give yourself (and others) time to integrate and process.

- It takes time. Recovery is a very individual experience.

- When necessary to tell, TELL. Telling doesn't mean reliving the emotions.

- Provide compassion and respect. Most of us, most of the time, are doing the best we can in the moment.

Closing Thoughts

In writing this book we hope you've heard us on multiple levels - both the Small Picture (practical, everyday level) and the Big Picture (on the level of Humanity).

We truly believe, at its most profound, that *Emotional First-Aid* is about our universal need for Safety and Compassion in action.

We're sure you've already observed a ripple effect that happens whenever caring, courageous people seek safety, solution and recovery with one another - their actions activate our own empathy system. In other words, simply observing others' compassionate and loving actions stimulates similar responses within us. From this place we find ourselves more motivated to join together and collectively effort to create emotional safety and support. That is what we believe creating a Heart-Mind connection and mindset is all about.

Since we became professional helpers, we've learned a few things. An important one we want to pass along to you now is this:

> **It Is NOT your job to fix people** - whether they are small or tall! - but rather to help them get to a point where they can receive support and access helpful resources; to offer your company and acceptance, as they return and restore themselves to wholeness; and later put that learned resilience into action for others.

You won't be surprised to hear we believe this particular path for helping works best when we begin from a place of heart-centeredness, an organically radiating energy, sending out ripples from both our individual and collective actions.

We've also observed that taking action from the heart-centered state creates more self-forgiveness and greater compassion, understanding and acceptance. This is of the highest importance for our children. Modelling this state and mindset of heart-centeredness is how children will learn from us. They are the ones who most need to feel safe, and trust that we have solutions for their troubles. They are learning from us that they can develop the skills to take care of themselves and from there become loving, caring, compassionate members of Humanity.

To that end, this book (and our comprehensive course - *see page 112*) all speak to the practical - the myriad things you can do, both in the moment and as troubling events pass, and how to harness your heart and mind to address the tasks before you in the world.

With kindness and appreciation for sharing this time with us, and receiving our information,
Deborah D Miller and Jondi Whitis

ALL OF THIS IS ABOUT creating a new humanity: a bigger message than simply getting through immediate panic and times of trouble.

What-to-Do-When Charts

Your What-to-Do-When Charts

Print out and laminate copies of the charts that follow, placing them in several places where they can be easily found and used.

Practicing these strategies create a solid foundation for long-term, sustainable emotional health and wellness.

What-to-Do-When Charts

JUST BEFORE
What Goes On
A primal or physical reaction, intuitive hit something's coming

What to Do/Recognize
Paying Attention & Preparing Phase: awareness & grounding

Little T Trauma and Intervention
4-7-8 Breathing   Shushing   Pretzel   Grounding   EFT

Big T Trauma and Intervention
3x3   Heart Breathing   Grounding   EFT

AS IT BEGINS
What Goes On
A sense of <u>uncertainty</u> of what is to come, and heightening of our body's sensory intake and response systems

What to do/Recognize
Heightened Awareness Phase

Little T Trauma and Intervention
Thumps   Grounding   Shushing   EFT

Big T Trauma and Intervention
Head Hold   Grounding   EFT

DURING
What Goes On
Immediate safety decision time. The key is to keep grounded. Return to a more conscious, thinking state, ask questions, and use previously practiced resources.

What to Do/Recognize
Keep grounded.
Add *Emotional First-Aid* practices to reduce emotional overwhelm, and make wiser choices of action.
Practice creates readiness.

Little T Trauma and Intervention
Grounding   Verbal First-Aid   EFT

Big T Trauma and Intervention
Verbal First-Aid   Finger Holds   Grounding
Monkey   Tension Tamer   EFT

What-to-Do-When Charts

JUST AFTER

What Goes On
How we best proceed after the initial danger or threat has much to do with the context of the situation.

What to Do/Recognize
Stabilize first, then assess further actions needed. The strategies below ground and sustain one's readiness for action.

Little T Trauma and Intervention

Verbal First-Aid	Soothers	Thumps	Butterfly
Tap-N-Breathe	Heel Stomps	Heel Clicks	EFT

Big T Trauma and Intervention

Verbal First-Aid	Finger Squeezes	Heel Stomps
Tension Tamer	Gamut Point	EFT

INITIAL RECOVERY

What Goes On
Once stabilized/grounded, seek more outside info before proceding. Address emotional & physical reactions from traumatic event. Deal with initial shocks, and emotional & physical responses.

What to Do/Recognize
In the long-term aftermath, recovery *is* possible. May take medication or surgery, and feature individual, group, or therapeutic counseling, supporting the release of deeper issues.

Little T Trauma and Intervention

Flow	Snap, Clap and Stomp	Head Hold	EFT

Big T Trauma and Intervention

Tension Tamer	Head Hold	Tap-N-Breathe	EFT

LONG-TERM RECOVERY

What Goes On
Time to determine what steps will ensure long-term recovery and *sustain* a state of well-being.

What to Do/Recognize
Notice long-term recovery signs and symptoms. Use Tapping and Trauma Tapping Techniques, etc. Seek well-trained support person in these trauma recovery interventions.

Little T Trauma and Intervention

EFT	Tap n Talk

Big T Trauma and Intervention

EFT	Tap n Talk	Tension Tamer

APPENDIX

Emotional First-Aid
A broad term for strategies and interventions that use our bodies' energetic systems to rapidly bring relief, re-balancing and recovery in response to any upsetting environmental or traumatic situation.

Grounding
Not to be confused with 'Earthing,' the concept of 'Grounding' is all about helping ourselves or others return to a state of mental, physical and emotional balance.

Since the beginning of recorded time, this has been equated with both breathing and bringing mental focus to a neutral or peaceful state.

The exercises provided in the Appendix and book are designed to quickly invoke this state of 'groundedness,' so that we can respond more quickly and wisely to a situation.

Soothing
The concept of soothing used in our book is about bringing comfort, consolation and relief to a rattled or overly-activated nervous system.

Combined with deep, slower breathing, it can help us quickly and readily attain a more resourceful state of being from which we can take the most productive action.

Breathing

While the concept of breathing may seem self-evident, when we talk about it in our book we mean using one's breath consciously to quickly regulate the nervous system and increase awareness.

Conscious breathing supports and enables the mind to more quickly and easily move to a calm and resourceful state, the very thing to create human resilience.

Natural human design

A concept, not a protocol, this refers to the way in which the human body is naturally designed to respond to danger or threat, and how our nervous system, sensory array, neurological pathways and resulting physical reactions are immediately integrated and mobilized into action.

We also refer to how our body, mind and conscious awareness is designed to retain and retrieve the memory and learning of impactful experiences, including traumatic ones.

Somatic experience

As the word *soma** suggests, this concept is focused upon the physical body's recording of, and responsiveness to its environment and experience.

The emerging field of Epigenetics and years of research into our autonomic nervous system (ANS) reveal the way in which our physical reactions are attuned and altered to better survive the external environment.

*so·ma - /ˈsōmə/; noun: Biology
noun: soma; plural noun: somas; the body as distinct from the soul, mind, or psyche.*

EFT

The Emotional Freedom Techniques are a set of tools developed for everyday use by anyone.

A natural multi-tasking protocol, that addresses the user's somatic, cognitive, neurological and nervous systems, as well as what we call the socio-emotional systems of the brain's limbic system.

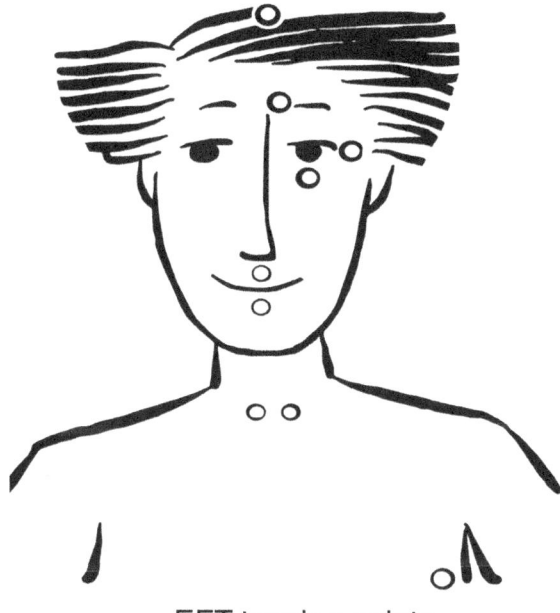

EFT tapping points

EFT is most often used to address the emotional underpinnings of our most common dilemmas and issues.

These include emotional overwhelm, worry, physical aches and pains, troubling thoughts or memories, and blocks to personal growth or development, such as limiting beliefs about one's self, others, the world, or expectations of Life.

Using a combination of mindful focus, acupressure stimulation, and limbic and nervous system down-regulation, EFT also uses an individual's verbalized assessment to specifically describe the troubling issue.

Here are easy-to-learn techniques for in-the-moment calming, soothing and re-balancing

FOR GROUNDING

Whale Breath, Dragon Breath, Volcano Breath

When we're afraid, our breath stays in the upper chest, where we can't hold very much air!

Instead, take a very deep breath, as if filling your belly with air, then blow it all out as you say HAAAAhhhhhhh!

If using the *whale breath* style, tilt your head upward like a 'whale' to release the air through your 'spout.'
- For the *dragon breath* style, thrust your head and 'paws' forward as you breathe out 'fire.'
- For the *volcano style*, lift head and arms up to 'explode' the air out of your lungs.
  - You may also choose to swing the arms down to the ground as you exhale.
  - Either is good for releasing the 'frozen' feeling in the diaphragm and jump-starting deeper breathing.

4-7-8 Breathing

Deepening your breathing by counting helps your nervous system regulate more quickly. Longer exhales are key to restoring deeper breathing and calm.

Try it now
1. Inhale to the count of 4
2. Hold the breath for the count of 7
3. Exhale fully to the count of 8
4. Repeat until relief is felt.

If you can't hold or exhale for this length of time, do shorter counts, simply ending with a longer exhale, until you can do the longer counts.

Shushing

1. Place your index finger vertically under the nose, covering your lips and chin.

2. Rest your thumb underneath the chin bone, curling the other fingers into your palm.

3. Breathe in and out through your nose for a full minute.

4. Then scan your body: notice how you've calmed yourself!

Tap-N-Breathe
1. Tap ANY of the EFT points while breathing slowly and deeply.
2. Add audible exhales or sighs to encourage deeper breathing, and model for others breathing slowly and deliberately.

FOR SOOTHING and GROUNDING

Comfort Hug
1. Place one of your hands across your torso, so that your palm cradles the ribs along the side of the body.
2. Place your other hand across your torso, resting on top of the first arm, lightly grasping the elbow.
3. Put the tip of your index finger into the natural 'notch' of the elbow.
4. Hold for a minute or two.
5. Notice how your breathing slows and deepens.
6. After a minute or two has passed, switch arm positions and hold for another minute or two.

Head Hold
1. Place one of your palms over your forehead.
2. With the other palm, cup the back of your head, just under the curve of the skull.
3. Hold this position for a minute or two as you breathe slowly and deeply, then switch hand positions.

The Pretzel

You can do this standing up or sitting down in a chair.

1. Stretch out legs, crossing one leg over the other.

2. Now stretch your arms out in front of you, crossing them, so that your hands are palm-to-palm.

3. Lace your fingers together, then swing your arms down, then raise them up towards the body, and into the chest.

4. Rest your interlaced hands and fingers upon your chest.

5. Hold this position as you breathe in and out for a minute or more.

6. Repeat, using the opposite leg and hands positions.

Extra help: When in the Pretzel position, press the tip of your tongue to the roof of your mouth. This helps ground one of the body's main energy pathways, the Governing Meridian.

FOR TRANSFORMING

Heart Breathing
1. Place one or both palms over the heart area.
2. Inhale to a count of 5, exhale for a count of 5.
3. Repeat until you feel calmer and more grounded.

Focusing your attention on your heart helps regulate your heart rate, and calms your mind.

You can heighten the experience by imagining something soothing or peaceful, or something that makes you feel grateful and loved.

Flow
Place both hands on your upper chest, then notice where your body is creating sensations, or giving you 'signals.'

Bring your awareness to the signal or sensation, then ask yourself:
- Where does that sensation or signal want to go?
- You might wish it to lift like fog, or flow it out from the top of your head like steam, cascade to the ground like a waterfall, or float away like a cloud.

Now ask yourself:
- Am I ready to let it go?
- When you're ready, let it go.

The Monkey

Younger children will especially appreciate this easy way to calm their energy.

1. With one palm flat on the chest, rub gently in a round or clockwise motion.

2. With the other palm, cover the belly button area and rub in an opposite circular motion.

Older kids and adults might prefer this version.

1. Place your middle finger inside the navel, gently pulling it up towards the the heart.

2. With your other hand, use the thumb and forefinger to gently massage the Collar Bone points in small circles.

3. Breathe slowly in this position for a minute or two before swapping hands to repeat the movements.

Finger Squeezes

1. Use one hand to surround and gently squeeze each finger of the other hand, one finger at a time.
2. Take your time, holding each finger in a firm squeeze, continuing to breathe, until you notice a gentle pulse sensation.

That's your heart beat!

3. Now release that finger and move to the next, squeezing it in the same fashion until the pulse sensation is felt.
4. Continue squeezing and breathing until each finger on one hand has been treated, then switch hands and repeat.

Soothers

1. While standing or sitting, cross both arms across your chest, placing your palms on your opposite upper arms, just below your shoulders.
2. With fingers lightly spread, stroke both arms in a downward motion from shoulders to elbows, and repeat.

Do the motion several times while slowly breathing in and out. Experiment with your breathing; inhale as you begin at the top of the arms, and exhale as the fingers move down the arms.

Butterfly

1. Cross your arms across your upper chest, placing your palms and fingers on the tops of your arms.
2. Slowly *alternate* lifting and lowering each hand up and down on your upper arms, one at a time, like butterfly wings flapping.

1. Flap hands like butterfly wings
2. Up and back down, flat on the upper arm
3. Alternate hand that's on top right/left

Use this movement with slow, deliberate breathing in and out to help you feel grounded.

Thumps

With a gentle, loosely closed fist, lightly and slowly thump the center of the upper chest while breathing.

If you imagine you are a baby gorilla, you'll know exactly how to do the thumps!

Alternate hands if you wish. Practice thumping slower and slower, as your inhales and exhales deepen. (Be creative! You might want to use memorable names, like *Chest Thumps, Tarzan Thumps*, etc.)

Heel Stomps
Stomp the heel of one of your feet, as you audibly exhale... hahhh, hahhh, hahhh.

Do at least 3 stomps and exhales per foot.
Then alternate feet.

Heel Clicks
1. With feet about two inches apart
2. Rise up on your toes and
3. Click your heels together 3-4 times, and
4. Return to the ground.

Now, add belly-breathing
1. As you rise onto your toes
2. Inhale into your belly.
3. Click your heels 3-4 times.
4. Exhale. Return your feet to the ground.

That's one round; repeat several times.

Snap, Clap and Stomp....Ahh!
1. Breathe.
2. Snap your fingers.
3. Clap your hands.

4. Then stomp your feet.
5. Exhale audibly.

Do this until you've created a satisfying, rhythm. Perform this with the child/children for at least a full minute.

Diverting the mind's attention to something actionable keeps both brain and body engaged; the rhythmic pattern is soothing and grounding to the nervous system, as well.

Tension Tamer
While focusing on a troubling event, situation or memory:
1. Tap along the side of your hand for about 12 counts.
2. Then Tap on these body points, in order:
>Eye Brows
>Side of Eye
>Under Eye
>Under Nose
>Under Lips
>Under Collar Bones
3. Then Tap across the nail beds of the fingers of one hand, in this order:
>Pinky
>Ring
>Middle
>Index
>Thumb

4. Tap again across and under the Collar Bone points.
5. Now breathe in and out very deliberately, twice.
6. Repeat the entire process.
7. Bring the troubling event lightly to mind again.
8. Notice any change, then repeat, if there is still a charge.

Gamut Point Tapping

Tap the acupuncture point located on the back of the hand, between the pinky and ring finger, about an inch below where the two fingers attach to the hand.

Tap gently and consistently for at least one minute as you slowly breathe in and out, more and more deeply.

As you can, elongate the exhale of your breath.

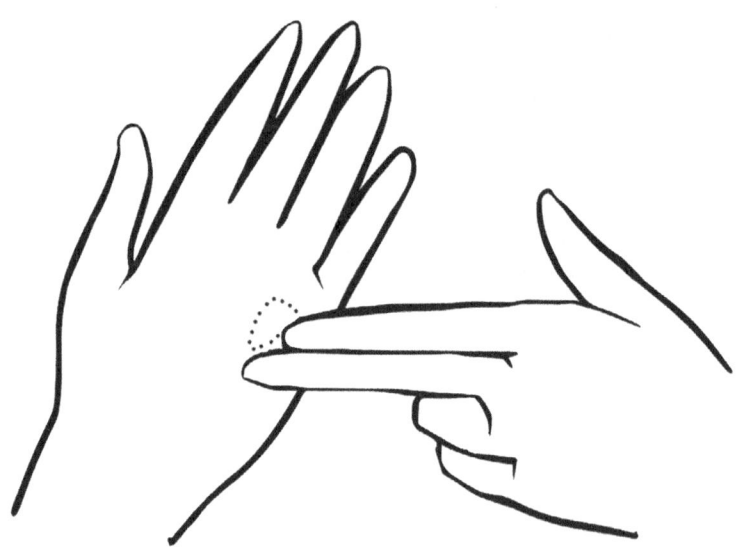

FOR CLARIFYING

3x3
1. Place your hands on your upper chest, one hand on top of the other.
2. Breathe in and out, slowly and deliberately, 3 times.
3. Ask a simple question, and allow a simple answer.
4. Then repeat back what was said, as in this example.

Your Question
"What are you feeling in your belly (or chest, etc.) right now?"
or...
"What's happening for you, right now?"

Child's Answer
"I'm mad."

Reflect their answer back to them, in this style:
"I'm okay, and I'm mad."

Repeat the breathing, questioning and answering procedure 3 times.

This will quickly show you what feelings and actions are causing the upset, so you can properly address them.

Tap n Talk
1. Focus on the child, bringing your full attention to the moment.
2. Ask them to simply breathe and follow along with you, as you gently Tap on the side of their hand or on the gamut point on the back of their hand.
3. After a minute or two, ask them to keep Tapping those points while they talk about whatever is happening for them in this moment, or about a recent event.
4. As you actively listen, reflect back to them just a word or phrase from their statements to let them know you are intently listening.
5. Allow the child to verbalize and release whatever they're struggling with by Tapping with them as they talk it out.

Verbal First-Aid
Verbal First-Aid is a method of communicating that quickly asks the child to follow simple directions or actions.

When humans are stressed or afraid, they have a more limited ability to follow directions or sort through incoming information. For this reason, we edit and shorten our language to help them more easily seek safety.

Examples
"Put on your coat."
"Follow me."
"Grab your classmate's hand."
"Hold this tightly."
"Wrap this around the cut, now."
"Wait here with Seth."
"Children: Hold hands. Walk outside with me."

ACKNOWLEDGMENTS

The following is a list of the original techniques that we've adapted from various energy psychology and medical experts.

- **Flow** is an adaptation of EmoTrance by Silvia Hartmann
- **Soothers** is an adaptation of Havening Technique by Dr. Ronald Ruden
- **3x3** is an adaptation of Dr. John Diepold's Heart Assisted Therapy (HAT)
- **The Pretzel** is an adaptation of Dr. Wayne Cook's Hook-Ups
- **Thumps** are adapted from Donna Eden's Energy Medicine
- **Finger Squeezes** are adapted from Jin Shin Jyutsu
- **Head Hold** is an adaptation from Tapas Fleming's TAT
- **Monkey** is an adaptation from Applied Kinesiology
- **Butterfly** is an adaptation of Daniel Benor's WHEE technique
- **Heart Breathing** is an adaptation of HeartMath's Heart Brain Coherence
- **Tension Tamer** is an adaptation of Trauma Tapping Technique (TTT) from Peaceful Heart.

These are just a few of the strategies and interventions in the full *Emotional First-Aid Course*, offered in-person, and online - you can read more about it on page 112.

Contact for classes and materials:
Jondi@JondiWhitis.com
Deborah@DeborahMiller.org

The Emotional First-Aid Course

The Emotional First-Aid Online Course is for those ready to go more deeply into the many specific concepts that help us understand how children thrive harsh situations, or how they may easily develop traumatic responses that could stay with them for years.

Our comprehensive course covers useful information to help you:
- Better understand crucial elements of childhood development
- Better understand the role of attachment issues
- Recognize the features of traumatic response
- Learn how the brain is designed to handle the sudden influx of incoming information in a threat response cycle
- Learn how to work in three systematic ways:
    - Cognitively, with the mindset and belief structure
    - Somatically, with the body's physical reaction capabilities
    - Emotionally, using knowledge about the triune brain, limbic and subconscious information systems
- Learn to use the many ways of creating safety and reassurance for children and youth.

Be a part of the solution by learning how to specifically support children's health and well-being in a challenging world.

More information about the *Emotional First-Aid Course*, offered both in-person and online, can be found at:
DeborahMiller.org/firstaidcourse

About the Authors

Jondi Whitis, MToT

Jondi Whitis is a well-known Master Trainer of Trainers for the original, non-profit global EFT association, *EFT International*. Based in New York, she travels widely to share her expertise and contagious enthusiasm for *Emotional First-Aid, Energy Psychology* and *EFT Tapping*.

Jondi's favorite work is helping children experience the world with less fear and suffering. She teaches them about their human design and how to use it, to better weather whatever Life throws at them. It's empowering to feel safe, seen and heard. She firmly believes we are stewards of the world's children, and that everyone can help our young ones better survive and more quickly recover after sudden, adverse situations - even from those of the past.

She has expanded her trainings to include and emphasize the importance of *Emotional First-Aid*, the first step in preventing and recovering from the everyday traumatic experiences that not only define our times, but can forever define children's meaning about themselves and the world. These lessons are combined with those of her co-author Deborah Miller, into an online course for those who feel the call to create even deeper understanding for helping our world's children to thrive.

As the former Lead Trainer for *the Newtown Community Trauma Relief Project*, Jondi learned how difficult it can be to manage our own distress through crises that literally affect everyone in the community.

This created a profound desire to help more children and their caregivers in this era of difficult, frequent and distressing challenges. Creating this handbook, *Emotional First Aid for Children*, with colleague Deborah D. Miller, PhD, has been a natural outpouring of that vision.

With this book's release, Jondi renews her intention to provide what she's learned to all who have, work with, and care for children, so they will have the information, tools and confidence to teach easily-learned and applied methods for rapid regulation, re-set and recovery.

Jondi welcomes invitations to speak on these issues and conduct customized trainings for a variety of issues and interests.

JondiWhitis.com
Jondi@EFT4Results.com

Jondi's creative resources for helpers and healers are available through Amazon:

How to Be A Great Detective, the Handy-Dandy Guide to Using Kindness, Compassion and Curiosity to Resolve Emotional, Mental & Physical Upsets for Tappers, Practitioners and Caregivers...

EFT Training for Mastery, the Handy-Dandy Guide for Creating Great Introductory Groups for Tappers, Practitioners & Helping Professions.

Deborah D. Miller, PhD

Deborah D. Miller has a PhD in Cell and Molecular Biology and is a Trainer and expert in EFT Tapping. She is also a Reiki Master, Life Transformed Coach™ and internationally-renowned author.

Since 2007, Deborah has been working with children suffering from cancer, helping them and their care-givers alleviate the fear, anxiety, and stress arising from serious illness, and to better understand the need to cleanse and nourish the physical body as an integral part of the healing process.

She also helps people recover from the trauma of natural disasters. Having lived through three major local earthquakes, herself, she now helps those around her navigate through and triumph over the inevitable emotional and physical aftermaths of sudden traumatic events.

Deborah's scientific knowledge, coupled with her continuing studies of Quantum Physics and Universal Truths enable her to better understand the physiological functions of the different tissues, organs and systems in the body and their corresponding emotional states. It's an integral part of her client support, helping them discover and release the underlying causes of emotional and physical traumas.

Deborah guides people to gently release their learned beliefs, habits, patterns and traumas in favor of healthier choices that create calm, joy, and inner peace. This unique blend of energy psychology, science, and spirituality enables her to apply and teach easily learned principles that provide relief and hope, even in traumatic situations.

Easing pain and emotional distress in children and adults, whether from an illness or a traumatic event, is what drives Deborah's unshakeable devotion to supporting those who are suffering with tools to navigate and self-empower – creating hope and well-being.

Deborah is the author of the beautifully illustrated book *The Dragon with Flames of Love: Helping Children with Serious Illness Improve the Quality of Their Lives*, dedicated to empowering anyone faced with the challenge of a serious illness to find relief and peace.

In her book, *Green Drink Red Drink*, she provides critical information and recipes on how to add healthy greens to your meals to support your health with nutrition.

Deborah offers individual and group sessions in person and online. Her services, materials and books are available in both English and Spanish.

DeborahMiller.org
Deborah@DeborahMiller.org

Made in the USA
Middletown, DE
27 June 2020

11413274R00076